GRAMMAR AND USAGE GUIDE

THE
WORLD
BOOK

Volume
7
GRAMMAR
AND
USAGE
GUIDE

Published by
World Book, Inc.
a Scott Fetzer company
Chicago

Staff

Publisher
William H. Nault

Editorial

Editor in Chief
Robert O. Zeleny

Executive Editor
Dominic J. Miccolis

Associate Editor
Maureen M. Mostyn

Senior Editor
Michael K. Urban

Contributing Editor
Sevasti Spanos

Production Editor
Elizabeth Ireland

Index Editor
Joyce Goldenstern

Permissions Editor
Janet T. Peterson

Editorial Assistant
Elizabeth Lepkowski

Art

Executive Art Director
William Hammond

Designers
Tessing Design, Inc.

Production Artist
Cynthia Schultz

Photography Director
John S. Marshall

Photographer
Don Sala

Product Production

Executive Director
Peter Mollman

Manufacturing
Joseph C. La Count, director

Research and Development
Henry Koval, manager

Pre-Press Services
Jerry Stack, director
Randi Park
Sandra Van den Broucke

Proofreaders
Marguerite Hoye, head
Ann Dillon
Esther Johns
Daniel Marotta

ISBN 0-7166-3191-1 (Volume 7)
ISBN-0-7166-3184-9 (set)
Library of Congress Catalog No. 86-50558
b/hf

Contents

Introduction

One of the most important skills you must master during your years in school is the ability to express yourself in writing. In order to achieve this goal, you must develop a strong knowledge of proper grammar and usage. This volume gives the information you need in order to put good grammar and usage to work for you.

The *Grammar and Usage Guide* is divided into four sections. The first section, "Grammar and Usage Guidelines," introduces the eight parts of speech: nouns, pronouns, adjectives, verbs, adverbs, prepositions, conjunctions, and interjections. Each part of speech is defined, and their various uses and functions within sentences are shown. The second section is entitled "Sentence-Building Guidelines." It explains how to link phrases and clauses together to form effective and grammatically correct sentences.

Are you having trouble deciding which words should be capitalized or which punctuation marks are needed in your writing? Refer to Section III, "Capitalization and Punctuation Guidelines," for help in these areas. Section IV contains many of the commonly misused words and constructions that can weaken your writing. Entitled "Common Grammar and Usage Errors," this final section also shows you how to correct and avoid many of the problems that students confront while writing.

The *Grammar and Usage Guide* serves as a ready reference for answering your questions on proper grammar and usage. Keep it close at hand when writing a paper, a report, or even when writing letters. The guidelines and rules in this volume will help you express yourself more clearly in writing, which should help you become a more successful student.

I GRAMMAR AND USAGE GUIDELINES

This section shows how to identify different types of words and how to put words together correctly. The eight parts of speech are defined, and rules and uses for each are given.

under **battalion** | ...
bat·tal·ion (bə tal'yən) *n* 1 a tactical unit made
up of a headquarters and two or more compa-
nies, batteries, or similar organizations it may be
part of a regiment. 2 any large group
that are administrative as well as tactical units
together. Abbr: bn. 3 an army ...
2 any large division of an army any large group
ers helped to rescue the flood victims
battalions a large number · battalions of teachers. The soldier-settlers ... came to plant bat-
Weekly) · battalions of coffee trees (Manchester Guardian

...

bathy·ther·mo·graph (bath'ə ther'mə graf)
...the sea and deep-sea life · [< Greek *bathys*
deep + English *sphere*]
bath·y·ther·mo·graph (bath'ə ...) *n*, an instrument for measuring the tem-
perature of the sea, especially at a deep level.
graph | [< Greek *bathys* deep + *thermē* heat + English
-graph]
ba·tik (bə tēk' bat'ik), *n*, *adj*, *v* — *n* 1 the art
and method of making designs on cloth by dye-
ing only part at a time, the rest being protected
by a removable coating of wax. 2 a cloth dyed in
this way. 3 a design formed in the way. 4 a design consisting of a medley of colors characteristic of or patterned on that of this art.
— *adj* 1 made by or of batik, made
2 like | [< Javanese *mbatik* writing, drawing]

...

These activities have been designed to review your
understanding of the commonly misused words, phrases...
structions presented in this section. Answers to the
...ies can be found in the **Answer Key** that

Correcting misspelled words

The following words are misspelled; write the correct spelling
for each word.

1. batallion
2. fam...
3. s...
4. ...
5. ...

6. priveledge
7. vascilate
8. questionaire
9. souvener
10. alledge

11. copywrited
12. protacol
13. superceed
14. appearence
15. extasy

...ised constructions

...ing sentences contains one or more misused
...ify the problems—for example, subject-
...ence, or misplaced modifier. Then

Co...

Each...
con...
verb...
rewr...

1. A...
2. Ea...
3. Be...
...rep...
4. I we...
...blo...
5. Tha...
...thin...
...wr...
...dis...

...correct word use

...ven in parentheses, choose the...
...s the best word use.
...beside) my husband...
...the living room, she...
...act and will (try to, ... expected, anticipated)...
...ney. Could you ... (credible, credi...
...causes cancer.
...to be

Grammar and Usage Guidelines

*G*rammar and usage guidelines show how to put words together correctly. Following these guidelines results in clear and effective writing and speaking. This section presents grammar and usage guidelines for each of the eight parts of speech: nouns, pronouns, adjectives, verbs, adverbs, prepositions, conjunctions, and interjections.

Nouns

A noun names a person, place, thing, idea, action, or quality.

Common and Proper Nouns

There are two kinds of nouns: common nouns and proper nouns. A common noun names a type of person, place, or thing. *Boy, animal, city, mountain, pencil, chair, flower, machine,* and *telephone* are all common nouns. A proper noun names a particular person, place, or thing. *John, Fido, San Francisco,* and *Mount Rushmore* are all proper nouns.

Abstract, Concrete, and Collective Nouns

Nouns can be divided into three other groups: abstract, concrete, and collective.

An abstract noun names things that cannot be seen or touched, such as qualities, actions, and ideas. *Courage, cleanliness, loyalty, greed, love,* and *danger* are all abstract nouns.

A concrete noun names things that can be seen and

touched. *Desk, tree, guitar, band, student, cup,* and *window* are all concrete nouns.

A collective noun names a group of people or things. *Team, flock, panel, audience, gang, class, herd,* and *jury* are all collective nouns.

When a collective noun refers to a group as a unit, any verbs and pronouns related to the noun are in the singular:

> The class *has gone* to the museum.
>
> The flock headed on *its* southward course in late October.

When a collective noun refers to the individual members of a group, any verbs and pronouns related to the noun are in the plural:

> The gang *are* all *going their* separate ways.
>
> The panel *are submitting their* opinions to the chairperson today.

Gender

All nouns have one of four genders: masculine, feminine, common, or neuter. Nouns that specify male creatures are masculine: *John, father, brother, king, rooster.* Nouns that specify female creatures are feminine: *Mary, mother, sister, queen, hen.*

Most nouns that name creatures give no indication of gender. These nouns are said to have common gender. *Child, animal, parent, relative, singer,* and *cook* are examples of common nouns. All nouns naming nonliving objects are called neuter. *Rock, candle, picture,* and *ribbon* are all examples of neuter nouns.

Noun endings such as *-ess, -trix,* and *-ine* can be added to nouns to make them feminine (poet*ess,* avia*trix*), but these endings are rarely used. Instead, nouns of common gender such as *poet* and *aviator* are used to refer to both sexes.

Some words that are masculine (*fireman, postman, policeman*) have alternatives with common genders (*fire fighter, mail carrier, police officer*). The use of common gender lessens the possibility of sexist interpretation.

Number

A noun's number shows whether the noun names one or more than one person or thing. A noun is singular if it names one person or thing: *child, rock, mouse.* A noun is plural if it names more than one person or thing: *children, rocks, mice.*

Most nouns change their form in the plural: *cat—cats; church—churches.* Most plurals can be formed simply by adding *-s* or *-es.* The spelling of some nouns changes to form the plural: *child—children; woman—women; mouse—mice; shelf—shelves; foot—feet.* The spelling of other nouns does not change at all in the plural: one *sheep*—two *sheep;* one *deer*—two *deer;* one *quail*—two *quail.* Consult your dictionary whenever you are in doubt about how to form noun plurals. Here are some more irregular ones:

Singular	Plural
alumnus (male)	alumnae
alumna (female)	
barracks	barracks
criterion	criteria
fungus	fungi
half	halves
loaf	loaves
louse	lice
man	men
ox	oxen
phenomenon	phenomena
self	selves
thesis	theses
tooth	teeth
wife	wives

Appositives

An appositive is a noun, or a group of words acting as a noun, that means the same thing, explains, or elaborates on the noun that comes before it.

Carol, my best *friend,* is moving to Toledo. (friend = Carol)

Lou's *neighbor, Chuck Matts,* won the school election. (Chuck Matts = neighbor)

Harry's long-standing *dream, to visit California,* finally came true. (to visit California = dream)

I enjoy playing two *sports, football and soccer.* (football and soccer = sports)

Possessive Case

Nouns change their form to show ownership: *Barbara's* gloves; the *baby's* bottle; the *scouts'* leader. These form changes show that the nouns are in the possessive case.

All singular nouns form the possessive by adding an apostrophe and *-s:*

Sally's coat
My brother's skates

Exception: Singular nouns that end in *-s* form the possessive by adding either an apostrophe and *-s* or an apostrophe only. Both forms of the possessive are considered correct:

Charles's book
Charles' book

Plural nouns that end in *-s* form the possessive by adding an apostrophe only:

The girls' dressing room
The boys' gym teacher

Plural nouns that do not end in *-s* form the possessive by adding an apostrophe and *-s:*

The men's hats
The children's toys

In cases of joint ownership, only the last word shows possession:

Jack and *Barbara's* dog
Mother and *Father's* car

When two or more persons own something individually, both words show possession:

> *Helen's* and *Linda's* books
> *Dorothy Johnson's* and *David Washington's* computers

In compound nouns (nouns made of more than one word), only the last word shows possession:

> father-in-*law's*
> editor in *chief's*

Pronouns

A pronoun takes the place of a noun. Pronouns stand for people or things without naming them.

There are five kinds of pronouns: personal, relative, demonstrative, indefinite, and interrogative.

Personal Pronouns

A personal pronoun's form shows whether the pronoun refers to a person speaking (first person), a person spoken to (second person), or a person or thing spoken about (third person). There is more than one spelling for each "person." Which one to use depends on which case is needed.

Singular

1st person	I	me	mine	my	myself
2nd person	you	you	yours	your	yourself
3rd person	he	him	his	his	himself
	she	her	hers	her	herself
	it	it	its	its	itself

Plural

1st person	we	us	ours	our	ourselves
2nd person	you	you	yours	your	yourselves
3rd person	they	them	theirs	their	themselves

Reflexive pronouns are formed by adding *-self* or *-selves* to some forms of the personal pronouns: *myself, yourself,* *himself, herself, itself, ourselves, yourselves, themselves.* These pronouns are called "reflexive" because they show that the verb's action is turned back on the word or words the reflexive pronouns stand for.

> My baby *brother* just learned how to feed *himself.*

Reflexive pronouns can emphasize the word or words they stand for.

> I spoke to *Jack* and *Alan themselves.*

Alert: A reflexive pronoun cannot be used alone. It must refer to someone or something.

Correct: *Todd* looked at *himself* in the mirror.
Incorrect: They asked *myself* and her to join them.

Relative Pronouns

Relative pronouns introduce adjective clauses. The relative pronouns are *who, whose, whom, which,* and *that.*

> Mr. Samuels is the architect *who* designed the school library.
> The mystery book, *which* was a gift from Claire's brother, held her spellbound from beginning to end.
> The committee *that* planned the project has been congratulated.

Demonstrative Pronouns

Demonstrative pronouns are used to designate particular people, places, or things that may or may not be named in the same sentence. The demonstrative pronouns are *this, that, these,* and *those.*

> Is *this* what you asked for?
> *That* is the *dog* I want.
> *These* are the best *cookies.*
> I want *those.*

Indefinite Pronouns

Indefinite pronouns refer to one or more persons or things in general. Some indefinite pronouns are:

all	both	everything	nobody	several
any	each	few	none	some
anybody	either	many	no one	somebody
anyone	everybody	most	one	someone
anything	everyone	neither	other	something

Is there *anything* I can do?
Please pass me a *few.*
We had to choose from among *several.*
Somebody has been here.

Interrogative Pronouns

Interrogative pronouns are pronouns used to ask questions. The interrogative pronouns are: *who, whom, whose, which,* and *what.*

Who is going to open the door?
Which of these kids have you met?
What is happening over there?

You have probably noticed that the same pronoun sometimes falls into more than one category. For instance, *who* can be a relative pronoun or an interrogative pronoun.

There's the girl *who* lives next door. (Relative pronoun)
Who wrecked the bike? (Interrogative pronoun)

To decide what to call a pronoun, look at its use in the sentence.

Case

Personal pronouns and the pronouns *who* and *whoever* change their form depending on how they are used in a sentence. These form changes show the case of the pronoun. There are three cases: nominative, objective, and possessive.

Nominative Case

I	we
you	you
he, she, it	they
who, whoever	

Pronouns used as subjects of sentences are in the nominative case.

> *I* went to the movies.
> *You* look tired.
> *We* students complained about the assignment.
> *Who* knows the answer?

Many people use the wrong pronoun form when a subject consists of more than one word. Remember: No matter how many nouns or pronouns are in the subject, the subject is always in the nominative case.

> *He* and *I* have been friends for years. (Not: *Him* and *I* or
> *Him* and *myself*)
> *You* and *she* are invited for dinner. (Not: *You* and *her*)
> *Martin* and *he* went to the game. (Not: *Martin* and *him*)

Pronouns used as predicate nominatives are in the nominative case.

> It was *I* who called.
> Someone left a book on the desk. Was it *you* or *he*?

Objective Case

me	us
you	you
him, her, it	them
whom, whomever	

Pronouns used as direct objects of verbs are in the objective case.

> Does Mark know that Cathy likes *him*?
> Mother wants *us* to come home for dinner.
> Jim and Sylvia were talking in class until Mr. Martin asked
> *them* to stop.
> *Whom* will you invite to your party?

Pronouns used as indirect objects are in the objective case.

> Uncle Charles and Aunt Sarah sent *me* a lovely birthday card.
> Cindy was happy when Dad gave *her* the car keys.
> Would you please tell *us* a story?
> When the Wilsons moved, we gave *them* a party.

Pronouns used as objects of prepositions are in the objective case.

> Deliver the package directly to *me,* please.
> Do you wish to go with *him?*
> Why doesn't anyone ever listen to *us?*
> To *whom* do you wish to speak?

Many people use the wrong pronoun form when direct objects, indirect objects, and objects of prepositions consist of more than one word. Remember: No matter how many nouns or pronouns form the direct, indirect, or prepositional object, they are all in the objective case.

> If you want to know the answer, just ask *Jack* and *me.* (Not: *Jack* and *I* or *Jack* and *myself*)
> Martha requested that all the survey responses be sent directly to *John* and *him.* (Not: *John* and *he*)
> The store never sent *Mother* and *her* the items they ordered. (Not: *Mother* and *she*)

A good way to test yourself in cases like these is to separate the noun and pronoun. Repeat the sentence using each pronoun to see which sounds best. For example, ". . . just ask *me*" sounds much better than ". . . just ask *I.*" Therefore, *Jack* and *me* is correct.

Pronouns used in incomplete constructions take either the objective or the nominative case, depending on the meaning of the sentence.

> Sally likes Margaret better than *me.* (Full construction: better than she likes *me*)
> Sally likes Margaret better than *I.* (Full construction: better than *I* do)

Possessive Case

my, mine	our, ours
your, yours	your, yours
his, her, hers, its	their, theirs

whose

Possessive pronouns indicate ownership. They can be used as predicate nominatives. In that case, they use the forms *mine, ours, yours, his, hers, its, theirs, whose.*

> This book is *mine.*
> The yellow sweater is *yours.*

Possessive pronouns can also be used as adjectives. In that case, they take the form *my, our, your, his, her, its, their, whose.*

> This is *my* book.
> *Whose* coat is that?

Alert: Never use an apostrophe with possessive pronouns.

The next move is *yours.*
(Not: *your's*)
The wind shifted *its* direction.
(Not: *it's,* which means *it is*)
That new speedboat is *ours.*
(Not: *our's*)
Whose dog was barking last night?
(Not: *who's,* which means "who is")
Theirs is the first house on the left.
(Not: *their's*)

Agreement

The noun a pronoun stands for is called its antecedent. A pronoun always agrees with its antecedent in person (first, second, or third person), number (singular or plural), and gender (masculine, feminine, or neuter). In the following examples, antecedents are marked (A), and pronouns are marked (P):

(A)   (P)

Sally gave *her* crayons to Judy.

(Third person, singular, feminine)

(A)   (P)

The *boy* bought *his* own lunch.

(Third person, singular, masculine)

(A)   (P)

Rick and Edna practiced *their* skating routine.

(Third person, plural)

(A)   (P)

I am having a hard time with *my* homework tonight.

(First person, singular)

When the antecedent is a collective noun, use either a singular or a plural pronoun, depending upon the sentence's meaning.

The *jury* are in the next room casting *their* votes.

(Each member of the jury is casting an individual vote.)

The *jury* met to reach *its* decision.

(The jury, acting as a unit, met in order to reach a decision.)

The indefinite pronouns *anybody, anyone, anything, each, either, everybody, everyone, everything, neither, nobody, none, no one, one, somebody, someone* and *something* are singular.

Each girl had *her* own gym locker.

Neither boy took *his* turn at bat.

Many people make mistakes in antecedent agreement when plural nouns come between the singular indefinite pronouns and pronouns that stand for them later in a sentence. Remember: These indefinite pronouns are singular no matter what words follow them, and so are the later pronouns.

One of the women lost *her* gloves.

Neither of the dogs got *its* shot this year.

When the antecedent of a pronoun refers to both men and women, or when the gender of an antecedent is unknown, the masculine singular pronoun may be used.

Everyone will get *his* turn to be class monitor.
Each person entering the theater had to show *his* ticket.

Some people are reluctant to follow this rule because they feel it fosters sexism. A good way to avoid the problem is to put the antecedent in plural form and make any necessary changes to the rest of the sentence.

All of the students will get *their* turn to be class monitor.

Or you can leave the antecedent alone and change another word in the sentence.

Everyone will get *a* turn to be class monitor.

You can also use masculine and feminine pronouns combined by a slash (*he/she, s/he, her/his*).

Everyone will get *his/her* (or *her/his*) chance to be class monitor.

Adjectives

An adjective modifies a noun or a pronoun.

Adjectives make the meaning of a noun or pronoun more specific by describing it or limiting it in some way. There are two types of adjectives: descriptive and limiting.

Descriptive Adjectives

A descriptive adjective indicates a noun's quality or condition.

The area was covered with *thick* vines.
The plants had *short* roots.
The trees were surrounded by *red* flowers.
High hills rose in the distance.

Limiting Adjectives

A limiting adjective points out a noun or indicates its number or quantity. Limiting adjectives can be classified as numerical adjectives, pronomial adjectives, or articles.

Numerical Adjectives

Numerical adjectives give number. There are two kinds of numerical adjectives: cardinal and ordinal.
Cardinal numbers answer "how many?"

> *Six* chairs were in the room.
> The table seats *eight* persons.
> The report contained *ten* pages.

Ordinal numbers answer "in what order?"

> The *second* step is broken.
> Our team came in *third*.
> The *fifth* carbon copy is hard to read.

Pronomial Adjectives

Many pronouns can be used as adjectives, in which case they are called pronomial adjectives. There are four kinds of pronomial adjectives: personal, demonstrative, indefinite, and interrogative.

Personal—my, your, his, her, our, their

> Here is *my* garden.
> Where is *your* scarf?
> John was listening to *his* radio.
> Sally lost *her* ring.
> Welcome to *our* home.
> Hank and Phyllis danced to *their* favorite song.

Demonstrative—this, that, these, those

> *This* time you've gone too far.
> *That* route is too long.
> *These* colors go well together.
> *Those* people are lost.

Indefinite—any, few, other, several, somebody

> Select *any* dessert you wish.
> *Few* people are so friendly as Martin.
> *Other* methods will work just as well.
> *Several* questions arose.
> *Somebody* from the group should go.

Interrogative—which, what

> *Which* song is number one?
> *What* day will you be here?

Articles

Some grammar experts consider both the definite and indefinite articles to be adjectives.

> *The* doctor came to our house. (definite article)
> *A* number of people complimented me on my baking. (indefinite article)

Placement of Adjectives

Adjectives usually come before the noun or pronoun they modify.

> She bought the *red* dress.
> We sat in the *warm* sun.
> The *skinny young* man always ate as much as he wanted.
> The *poor* woman wore a *torn, rumpled* coat.

Adjectives can be placed after the noun or pronoun for variety or emphasis. In this case, the adjective is said to be in apposition to the noun or pronoun.

> The mountain climber, *exhausted,* paused in the shelter.
> The dog, *lean* and *alert,* led the search party.
> The house, *old* and *neglected,* had stood vacant for years.

Comparison of Adjectives

Descriptive adjectives modify nouns and pronouns by indicating their qualities and characteristics. The degree to which nouns and pronouns have the quality or characteristic can be indicated by means of comparison. Adjectives can be compared in ascending (upward) or descending (downward) order.

There are three degrees of comparison: positive, comparative, and superlative. The positive degree does not actually compare. It expresses the quality or characteristic:

tall, attentive, good. The comparative degree expresses a degree higher or lower than the positive: *taller, less tall, more attentive, less attentive, better, worse.* The superlative degree expresses the highest or lowest degree of the quality or characteristic: *tallest, least tall, most attentive, least attentive, best, worst.* There are three ways of forming the comparison upward:

1. Some adjectives form the comparative by adding *-er* for the comparative degree and *-est* for the superlative degree. Almost all adjectives of one syllable and some adjectives of two or more syllables form the comparative this way.

Positive	Comparative	Superlative
short	shorter	shortest
smart	smarter	smartest
tall	taller	tallest
tender	tenderer	tenderest

2. Most adjectives of two or more syllables form the comparative by using the words *more* and *most.*

Positive	Comparative	Superlative
attentive	more attentive	most attentive
reasonable	more reasonable	most reasonable
stubborn	more stubborn	most stubborn

3. Some adjectives form their comparatives irregularly. The most common of these include:

Positive	Comparative	Superlative
bad/ill	worse	worst
good/well	better	best
far	farther	farthest
little	less	least
many/much	more	most

To indicate comparison downward, all adjectives use the words *less* and *least.*

Positive	Comparative	Superlative
reasonable	less reasonable	least reasonable
stubborn	less stubborn	least stubborn
tall	less tall	least tall

Never use *more* and *most* when adding *-er* and *-est* to adjectives. This is a double comparison and should be avoided.

Incorrect: Sandra was *more smarter* than Caroline.
Correct:　Sandra was *smarter* than Caroline.

Incorrect: Harold is the *most tallest* person I know.
Correct:　Harold is the *tallest* person I know.

Choice of Adjectives

Avoid unnecessary, vague, and repetitious adjectives. They weaken the descriptive power of your writing and speaking. Adjectives should make descriptions sharper and more interesting.

Unnecessary adjective: We visited the observation tower on top of the *tall*, 110-story building. (Any 110-story building is tall. Adding the adjective *tall* gives no additional information.)

Vague adjectives: Debbie is one of the *nicest* people I have ever met. (The sentence gives no information about what makes Debbie so special. Is she kind? Polite? Helpful? Avoid using *nice*. Be specific.)

Repetitious adjectives: A *big, huge* truck drove by and splashed water all over my new coat. (Delete *big* or *huge*. They mean almost the same thing.)

Predicate Adjectives

A predicate adjective is an adjective that follows a linking verb. Linking verbs include all forms of the verb *to be: am, are, is, was, were*. Other linking verbs include: *appear, feel, grow, look, seem, smell, sound*, and *taste*. They tell about the subject's state of being. They connect the subject to the adjectives or nouns that follow.

Because many linking verbs can also be used as action verbs (verbs that tell about a physical or mental occurrence), many people make the mistake of using an adverb after a linking verb. But a modifier following a linking verb is always an adjective, never an adverb.

Incorrect: That soup tastes *strangely.*
Correct: That soup tastes *strange.*

Incorrect: I feel *badly* when you leave.
Correct: I feel *bad* when you leave.

To test whether to use an adjective or an adverb, ask "Which word is being modified?" If the verb is being modified, use an adverb. If the subject is being modified, use an adjective.

The children grew *tall.*
(The adjective *tall* modifies the subject *children.*)

The children grew *quickly.*
(The adverb *quickly* modifies the verb *grew.*)

Ms. Johnson appeared *worried* when she heard the news.
(The adjective *worried* modifies the subject *Ms. Johnson.*)

Ms. Johnson appeared *suddenly* from behind the house.
(The adverb *suddenly* modifies the verb *appeared.*)

Common Errors

This/that—These/those

The pronomial adjective always agrees in number with the noun it modifies:

This (singular) *kind* (singular) of weather
That (singular) *sort* (singular) of book

Those (plural) *kinds* (plural) of songs
These (plural) *sorts* (plural) of exercises

Alert: Do not use *a* after kind and sort.

Incorrect: That sort of *a* cake.
Correct: That sort of cake.

Few/fewer—little/less

Few and *fewer* answer the question "How many?" (Can you count them?)

I have a *few* errands to run. (You can count the errands.)

Marcy has *fewer* records than Tracy. (You can count the records.)

Little and *less* answer the question "How much?" (These you cannot count.)

Ms. Marks has *little* patience with students who talk in class.
My sister has *less* time to spend with me now that she has a part-time job.

Verbs

A verb expresses an action or a state of being.

Action verbs show physical and mental actions. Some examples of action verbs are: *run, talk, sing, make, believe, think, hope, desire.* State-of-being verbs show a condition. Some examples of state-of-being verbs are: *appear, be, become, feel,* and *seem.*

Transitive and Intransitive Verbs

Transitive Verbs

There are other ways to classify verbs. A transitive verb, for example, shows action that is performed on something. Something receives the action. Each of these sentences contains a transitive verb:

John *hit* the ball to Michael.
(The ball received the hitting.)

Margaret *writes* letters to her cousins.
(The letters receive the writing.)

Mark and Sally *love* their mother.
(Mother receives the loving.)

Direct Object. The verbs above are transitive because they take a direct object. A direct object names the person or thing that receives the action of the verb. In the first sentence above, the direct object is the noun *ball,* which receives the action of the verb *hits.* In the second sentence, the direct object is the noun *letters,* which receives the action of the verb *write*. In the third sentence, the direct object is the noun *mother,* who receives the action of the verb *love*.

An easy way to find the direct object in a sentence is to find the subject and verb and then ask "whom?" or "what?". In the first sentence, you would ask, "John hit *whom* or *what*?" In the second, you would ask, "Margaret writes *what*?" In the third, you would ask, "Mark and Sally love *whom* or *what*?" In each case, the noun that answers the question is the direct object.

Indirect Object. Transitive verbs can also take indirect objects. An indirect object names the person or thing the action of the verb is performed toward or for. Each of these sentences contains both a direct object and an indirect object:

> John threw the *dog* a *bone.*
> Jennifer sent her *friend* a *letter.*
> Martha gave her *mother* some *perfume.*

In the first sentence, the indirect object is *dog* and the direct object is *bone.* (Ask: "John threw *what* to *whom* or *what*?") In the second sentence, the indirect object is *friend* and the direct object is *letter.* (Ask: "Jennifer sent *what* to *whom* or *what*?") In the third sentence, the indirect object is *mother* and the direct object is *perfume.* (Ask: "Martha gave *what* to *whom* or *what*?")

Intransitive Verbs

An intransitive verb takes no direct object. Each of these sentences contains an intransitive verb:

> Mark *sings* in the school choir.
> Harriet *walks* in the woods.
> Our baby brother *sleeps* through the night.

Transitive or Intransitive?

Many verbs can be either transitive or intransitive, depending on how they are used in the sentence. Remember: If a verb takes a direct object, it is a transitive verb. If it does not take a direct object, it is an intransitive verb.

Mary *writes* a letter. (transitive—direct object is *letter*)
Mary *writes* beautifully. (intransitive—no direct object)

John *walked* his dog. (transitive—the direct object is *dog*)
John *walked* to the store. (intransitive—no direct object)

I *read* three books a week. (transitive—direct object is *books*)
I *read* quickly. (intransitive—no direct object)

Linking Verbs

A linking verb is an intransitive, state-of-being verb that needs an adjective, noun, or pronoun to complete its meaning. The most common linking verb is *to be* in all its forms. Other common linking verbs are: *act, appear, feel, grow, look, seem, sound, taste,* and *turn.*

Jack *seems* sad.
The chocolate cake baking in the oven *smells* delicious.
George *will be* a professor.
That person in the gray hat *is* our lawyer.

Each of these sentences tells about a state of being. The verbs—*seem, feel, smell, be*—link the subjects with the adjectives or nouns that describe them. The adjectives or the nouns that follow linking verbs are closely related to the subject. In fact, they describe, define, or explain the subject. Most linking verbs can also be used as action verbs (verbs that show physical and mental action).

The hour *grew* late. (linking verb)
The children *grew* quickly. (action verb)
Harold *appeared* satisfied with our answer. (linking verb)
Ms. Robinson *appeared* at the door soon after the mail carrier rang. (action verb)

Adjectives that follow linking verbs are called predicate adjectives. Nouns that follow linking verbs are called predicate nominatives.

Joyce looks *pretty.* (predicate adjective)
The radio sounds *funny.* (predicate adjective)
Clarence became a *doctor.* (predicate nominative)
Marsha was a *leader.* (predicate nominative)

Voice

All transitive verbs can have two voices: active or passive. In the active voice, the subject of the verb performs the action. In the passive voice, the subject of the verb receives the action.

> John hit the ball. (active voice; subject—John)
> The ball was hit by John. (passive voice; subject—ball)
>
> A local company performed the opera. (active voice; subject—company)
> The opera was performed by a local company. (passive voice; subject—opera)

Notice what has happened in these four sentences. *Ball,* the direct object in the first sentence, has become the subject in the second sentence. *Opera,* the direct object in the third sentence, has become the subject in the fourth sentence. Sentences can be transformed from the active voice to the passive voice by turning the direct object into the subject.

The passive voice is formed by using an appropriate form of the verb *to be,* plus the past participle of the principal verb: The ball *is hit;* The ball *was hit;* The ball *will be hit;* The ball *will have been hit,* for example.

Mood

A verb's mood shows attitude or viewpoint. There are three moods: indicative, imperative, and subjunctive. Use the indicative mood for a statement or question of fact.

> You *are* serious about this?
> Ned *is learning* how to tap-dance.
> *Did* you *look at* the beautiful antique cars on display?

Use the imperative mood for a request or a command.

> Please *be* serious.
> *Learn* how to tap-dance.
> *Look at* those beautiful antique cars!

Use the subjunctive mood when the action or state of being is doubtful, conditional, unreal, or improbable.

If you *were* serious, I'd be.

Ned *should learn* to tap-dance.

Should you *look at* the antique cars, be sure to notice the
bumpers.

Person and Number

A verb's person and number depend on the subject. But in
almost all verbs, only the third person singular changes
form to show person and number.

Person depends on whether the subject is the person
speaking (first person), the person spoken to (second person), or the person spoken about (third person).

First person	Second person	Third person
I go, we go	you go	he goes
I walk, we walk	you walk	she walks
I am, we are	you are	it is

The number depends on whether the verb refers to a singular or plural subject.

Singular	Plural	Singular	Plural
I go	we go	I am	we are
you go	you go	you are	you are
he goes	they go	she is	they are

Tense

A verb's tense shows the time of the verb's action. There
are three major divisions of time: past, present, and future.
In each of these time frames, the action can be considered
simple (occurring at that particular moment) or perfect
(completed, or "perfected"). There are six tenses in English: present, present perfect, past, past perfect, future, and
future perfect.

Present Tense

—shows action occurring in the present:

I *see* my sister playing in the schoolyard.

The fire fighters *hear* the alarm and spring into action.

—shows habitual or customary action:

> Jim *walks* his dog every morning before school.
> My brother *talks* in his sleep.

—shows unchanging conditions, facts, or beliefs:

> One plus one *equals* two.
> Congressional elections *are held* every two years.
> When it *rains*, it *pours*.

—shows action completed in the past (called the historical present and used when the writer or speaker wants to make an especially vivid impression):

> Then on December 16, about 45 Bostonians dressed as Indians *raid* three British ships and *throw* 340 chests of tea into Boston Harbor. The Revolutionary War in America *is coming* closer now. It finally *begins* on April 19, 1775. This time, the place *is* Lexington, Massachusetts.

—shows action that will occur:

> She *flies* to Houston tomorrow.
> He *signs* the contract next week.

Present Perfect Tense

—shows action begun in the past and completed by the present moment:

> Jerry *has taken* all the required courses.
> I *have seen* the play that was recently made into a television special.

—shows action begun in the past and continuing up to or through the present moment:

> Cynthia *has been* my friend since the first day she moved to town.
> Harry *has been shooting* baskets for at least a half hour.

Past Tense

—shows action completed in the past:

> We *went* to the movies yesterday.
> I *enjoyed* meeting your cousin.

Past Perfect Tense

—shows an action that occurred in the past prior to another past action or event:

> Mark *had finished* drying the dishes by the time Sam arrived.
>
> I *had heard* good things about you long before I met you.

Future Tense

—shows an action that will occur in the future:

> They *will call* you later this afternoon.
>
> Martin *will visit* his aunt next month.

Future Perfect Tense

—shows an action that will be completed at some future time:

> Sandra *will have finished* two years of college by the time you see her this summer.
>
> We *will* already *have left* for our vacation before Saturday.

Verb Phrases

Frequently, a combination of verbs is needed to show tense, voice, and mood. (I *will go* to the store this afternoon; The game *was enjoyed* by all; I *might decide* not to go to the party.)

These groups of two or more verbs are called verb phrases. Verb phrases consist of a form of the principal, or main, verb plus one or more auxiliary, or helping, verbs.

Principal (Main) Verb

In verb phrases, the principal verb usually takes the form of the present or past participle. The present participle of a verb ends in *-ing;* for example, *seeing; hearing; speaking.* The past participle ends in *-d, -ed, -t, -en,* or *-n;* for example, *walked; left; stolen.*

Auxiliary (Helping) Verb

The most common auxiliary verbs are: *be, can, could, do, have, may, might, must, shall, should, will,* and *would.* (The verbs *be, do,* and *have* can also act as principal verbs. For instance: "I am a student"; "You do your best"; "We have three books." The other auxiliary verbs, such as *could, might, should,* and *would,* are sometimes called modal verbs.)

Note: The entire verb phrase is considered to be a sentence's verb. For example, in the sentence, *I have seen the Grand Canyon,* the verb is *have seen.* In the sentence, *I will have finished my book report by Friday,* the verb is *will have finished.* Word placement has no effect on what makes up the verb. In the sentence, *I will certainly have decided by Friday,* the verb is *will have decided.*

Principal Parts

Every verb has three principal parts: the present infinitive (usually called "the present"), the past indicative (usually called "the past"), and the past participle. Regular verbs form the past and the past participle by adding *-d* or *-ed* to the present infinitive.

Present	Past	Past participle
walk	walked	walked
look	looked	looked
dance	danced	danced
close	closed	closed

Verbs that form the past tense and/or the past participle in any other way are called irregular verbs.

Present	Past	Past participle
eat	ate	eaten
mean	meant	meant
sit	sat	sat
speak	spoke	spoken
write	wrote	written

Here is a list of some of the most common irregular verbs. To find any others, look in your dictionary. Each will be featured either in the dictionary's irregular verb list or individually in main entries that show the principal parts.

Present	Past	Past participle
be	was	been
beat	beat	beaten
become	became	become
begin	began	begun
bend	bent	bent
bind	bound	bound
blow	blew	blown
break	broke	broken
bring	brought	brought
build	built	built
burn	burned/burnt	burned/burnt
buy	bought	bought
catch	caught	caught
choose	chose	chosen
come	came	come
dive	dived/dove	dived
do	did	done
draw	drew	drawn
drink	drank	drunk
drive	drove	driven
eat	ate	eaten
fall	fell	fallen
fight	fought	fought
flee	fled	fled
fly	flew	flown
forbid	forbade	forbidden
freeze	froze	frozen
get	got	got/gotten
give	gave	given
go	went	gone
grow	grew	grown
hang (suspend)	hung	hung
hang (execute)	hanged	hanged
hide	hid	hidden/hid
hold	held	held
know	knew	known
lay (put or place)	laid	laid

Present	Past	Past participle
lead	led	led
lend	lent	lent
lie (recline; remain in position)	lay	lain
lie (tell a lie)	lied	lied
lose	lost	lost
make	made	made
mean	meant	meant
pay	paid	paid
ride	rode	ridden
ring	rang	rung
rise	rose	risen
run	ran	run
say	said	said
see	saw	seen
shake	shook	shaken
shrink	shrank/shrunk	shrunk/shrunken
sing	sang	sung
sink	sank	sunk
sit	sat	sat
sling	slung	slung
sow	sowed	sown/sowed
speak	spoke	spoken
spring	sprang	sprung
steal	stole	stolen
sting	stung	stung
swear	swore	sworn
swim	swam	swum
swing	swung	swung
take	took	taken
teach	taught	taught
tear	tore	torn
throw	threw	thrown
wake	woke/waked	woken/waked
wear	wore	worn
weave	wove	woven
wring	wrung	wrung
write	wrote	written

Conjugation

A verb's conjugation is a complete listing of all its forms by mood, number, person, tense, and voice. All the verb's forms come from its three principal parts (present, past, and past participle), combined with auxiliary verbs as needed.

Here is the complete conjugation of the verb *to see* in the active voice:

Indicative Mood

Singular	Plural	Singular	Plural
Present tense		**Present perfect tense**	
I see	we see	I have seen	we have seen
you see	you see	you have seen	you have seen
he, she, it sees	they see	he, she, it has seen	they have seen
Past tense		**Past perfect tense**	
I saw	we saw	I had seen	we had seen
you saw	you saw	you had seen	you had seen
he, she, it saw	they saw	he, she, it had seen	they had seen
Future tense		**Future perfect tense**	
I shall see	we shall see	I shall have seen	we shall have seen
you will see	you will see	you will have seen	you will have seen
he, she, it will see	they will see	he, she, it will have seen	they will have seen

Subjunctive Mood

Singular	Plural	Singular	Plural
Present tense		**Present perfect tense**	
(if) I see	(if) we see	(if) I have seen	(if) we have seen
(if) you see	(if) you see	(if) you have seen	(if) you have seen
(if) he, she, it sees	(if) they see	(if) he, she, it has seen	(if) they have seen
Past tense		**Past perfect tense**	
(if) I saw	(if) we saw	(if) I had seen	(if) we had seen
(if) you saw	(if) you saw	(if) you had seen	(if) you had seen
(if) he, she, it saw	(if) they saw	(if) he, she, it had seen	(if) they had seen

Subjunctive Mood (continued)

Singular	Plural	Singular	Plural
Future tense		**Future perfect tense**	
(if) I should see	(if) we should see	(if) I should have seen	(if) we should have seen
(if) you should see	(if) you should see	(if) you should have seen	(if) you should have seen
(if) he, she, it should see	(if) they should see	(if) he, she, it should have seen	(if) they should have seen

Imperative Mood

(you) see—singular and plural

	Present	Past	Perfect
Infinitive form:	to see		to have seen
Participle:	seeing	seen	having seen
Gerunds:	seeing		having seen

Synopsis

A conjugation's synopsis is a summary of a verb's forms in only one person. Here is a synopsis of *to see* in the passive voice, first person singular:

Indicative Mood

Present tense:	I am seen
Past tense:	I was seen
Future tense:	I shall be seen
Present perfect tense:	I have been seen
Past perfect tense:	I had been seen
Future perfect tense:	I shall have been seen

Subjunctive Mood

Present tense:	(if) I be seen
Past tense:	(if) I were seen
Future tense:	(if) I should be seen
Present perfect tense:	(if) I have been seen
Past perfect tense:	(if) I had been seen
Future perfect tense:	(if) I should have been seen

Imperative Mood

(you) be seen—singular and plural

	Present	Past	Perfect
Infinitive form:	to be seen		to have been seen
Participle:	being seen	seen	having been seen
Gerund:	being seen		having been seen

Conjugation of Progressive Forms

Each verb form suggests a different shade of meaning. The tables you just reviewed show conjugations of simple forms.

Another important form is the progressive form, which shows continuous action. Here is a synopsis of the progressive forms of *to see* in the active voice, first person singular.

Indicative Mood

Present tense:	I am seeing
Past tense:	I was seeing
Future tense:	I shall be seeing
Present perfect tense:	I have been seeing
Past perfect tense:	I had been seeing
Future perfect tense:	I shall have been seeing

Subjunctive Mood

Present tense:	(if) I be seeing
Past tense:	(if) I were seeing
Future tense:	(if) I should be seeing
Present perfect tense:	(if) I have been seeing
Past perfect tense:	(if) I had been seeing
Future perfect tense	(if) I should have been seeing

Imperative Mood

(you) be seeing—singular and plural

Alert: Do not confuse verb phrases in the progressive conjugation with the present participle used as an adjective.

I *am singing.* (verb phrase in progressive conjugation)
The *singing* bird nested in the tree. (present participle used as an adjective)

Verbals

Verbals are verb forms that can be used as parts of speech other than verbs. There are three kinds of verbals: infinitives, participles, and gerunds.

Infinitive

The infinitive, a verb's basic form, often follows the preposition *to*: *to walk, to go, to see.* It is in this form that the infinitive (*walk, go, see*) acts as a verbal.

As a noun:	*To err* is human. (Infinitive used as the subject of a sentence)
	I want *to go.* (Infinitive used as a direct object)
	Her main goal, *to win,* is unrealistic. (Infinitive used as an appositive)
As an adjective:	Here is a book *to read.* (Infinitive used to modify the noun *book*)
	Our vacation was a time *to relax.* (Infinitive used to modify the predicate nominative *time*)
As an adverb:	That is easy *to say.* (Infinitive used to modify the predicate adjective *easy*)
	John played *to win.* (Infinitive used to modify the verb *played*)

Notice that although the infinitive acts as a noun and is the subject of the sentence in the following examples, it keeps some verb characteristics. For instance, it can take a direct object.

> *To play the piano* was his greatest desire.
> (infinitive: *to play;* direct object: *piano*)

Or it can be modified by an adverb.

> *To run quickly* is difficult.
> (infinitive: *to run;* adverb: *quickly*)

Participle

Every verb has two participles: a past participle and a present participle. The past participle usually ends in *-ed, -d, -t, -en,* or *-n;* for example, *walked, chosen.* The present participle always ends in *-ing;* for example, *singing, dancing.*

Participles have two uses. Sometimes they are part of verb phrases (for example: I *am singing;* you *had gone*). Sometimes they act as adjectives. Participles that act as adjectives are verbals.

> Carole calmed the *frightened* kitten.
> (Past participle used as an adjective)

> Do you like *baked* potatoes?
> (Past participle used as an adjective)

> *Burning* leaves smell good.
> (Present participle used as an adjective)

> The *chirping* birds woke us up early.
> (Present participle used as an adjective)

Notice that although the past and present participles act as adjectives, they keep some verb characteristics. For instance, they can take an object.

> The girl *painting the fence* is my sister.
> (present participle: *painting;* direct object: *fence*)

Or they can be modified by an adverb.

> The *modestly bowing* violinist appreciated the audience's applause.
> (present participle: *bowing;* adverb: *modestly*)

Gerund

A gerund is a verb form ending in *-ing* that acts as a noun.

> *Swimming* is good exercise.
> (Gerund acting as the subject)

> I enjoy *hiking.*
> (Gerund acting as a direct object)

> My favorite sport, *fencing,* keeps me in shape.
> (Gerund acting as an appositive)

Notice that although the gerund acts as a noun, it also keeps some verb characteristics. For instance, it can take an object.

> I enjoy *singing folk songs.*
> (gerund: *singing;* object: *folk songs*)

Or it can be modified by an adverb.

> *Walking briskly* is healthy.
> (gerund: *walking;* adverb: *briskly*)

Gerunds and present participles both have *-ing* endings. Be careful to name them properly when analyzing sentences. A gerund acts as a noun. A present participle can act as an adjective.

> I like *swimming.*
> (Gerund used as a noun)

> The *swimming* children frolicked in the pool.
> (Present participle used as an adjective)

Agreement

Verbs agree in person and number with their subjects.

> *Harry runs* a mile a day.
> (Third person singular subject: *Harry*
> Third person singular verb: *runs*)

> *We run* to the store after school.
> (First person plural subject: *We*
> First person plural verb: *run*)

Singular verbs are used with these indefinite pronouns: *anybody, anyone, anything, each, either, everybody, every-*

one, everything, neither, nobody, none, no one, one, some-body, someone, something.

> *Each* apartment *has* a separate heating unit.
> *Neither* boy *wants* to run the errand.

Alert: Always use singular verbs with these pronouns. Don't become confused when the pronouns and the verbs are separated by phrases or clauses with plurals.

Each of the apartments *has* a separate heating unit.
Neither of the boys who are waiting *wants* to run the errand.

Compound subjects (two or more nouns used as the subject) usually take a plural verb.

> *Melissa and Charles plan* to be married in June.
> *Mother and Father go* out every Saturday night.

When the parts of a compound subject are thought of as one unit, they take a singular verb.

> *Peanut butter and jelly is* my favorite sandwich spread.
> The traffic's *hustle and bustle gets* on my nerves.

Compound subjects joined by the words *or, either . . . or,* and *neither . . . nor* take a singular verb unless the second subject is plural.

> *Either* Becky *or* Linda *wins* every prize.
> *Neither* Harry *nor* Cathy *wants* to dry the dishes.
> Sam *or* Kevin *has* the key.
> Jenny *or* the boys *have* the car.

Consistent Tense

Be sure that all verb tenses in a sentence are consistent. Actions happening at the same time should be in the same tense.

> **Incorrect:** John *walked* into study hall and *starts* complaining about his grade on the spelling test.
>
> **Correct:** John *walked* into study hall and *started* complaining about his grade on the spelling test.

Sometimes sentences describe actions happening at different times. Make sure the tenses represent the sequence of events correctly.

Incorrect:	He already *left* by the time I *arrived.*
Correct:	He *had* already *left* by the time I *arrived.*
Incorrect:	Elaine *has promised* to call when she *got* home.
Correct:	Elaine *has promised* to call when she *gets* home.

Adverbs

An adverb modifies a verb, an adjective, or another adverb.

Classifying Adverbs by Meaning

Adverbs usually answer the questions How? When? Where? or To what extent?

Mark walked *slowly.*
(Slowly modifies the verb, telling *how* Mark *walked.)*

I will leave *soon.*
(Soon modifies the verb, telling *when* I *will leave.)*

Let's go *out.*
(Out modifies the verb, telling *where* we shall *go.)*

Sally is *not* late.
(Not modifies the adjective, telling *to what extent* Sally is *late* [not at all].)

The elderly man moved *somewhat* gingerly.
(Quite modifies the adverb, telling *to what extent* the elderly man moved *gingerly.)*

Adverbs that tell *how* are called adverbs of manner. Some examples are: *beautifully, energetically, fast, happily, quickly.*

Adverbs that tell *when* are called adverbs of time. Some examples are: *before, later, now, soon, then.*

Adverbs that tell *where* are called adverbs of place. Some examples are: *down, forward, in, near, out, there, up.*

Notice that some adverbs of place can also act as prepositions.

> Let's climb *up.* (adverb)
> The kitten climbed *up* the tree. (preposition)

Adverbs that tell *to what extent* are called adverbs of degree. Some examples are: *almost, extremely, quite, rather, somewhat, very.*

Classifying Adverbs by Use

Adverbs of manner, time, place, and degree are classified by their meaning. Another way to classify adverbs is by their use.

Interrogative adverbs introduce questions. Some examples are: *how, when, where,* and *why.*

> *When* did you go?
> *Where* have you been?

Relative adverbs introduce subordinate clauses. Some examples are: *when, where, why.*

> I will meet you *when* classes are over.
> Do you know *why* Max was so angry?

Conjunctive adverbs (sometimes called transitional adverbs) join two independent clauses or two sentences, and modify one of them. Some examples are: *hence, however, moreover, nevertheless, otherwise, still, therefore, thus.*

> We followed the recipe; *however,* the casserole was not so
> good as we'd hoped.
> Sarah liked the dress; *nevertheless,* she did not buy it.

Independent adverbs have no grammatical function in a sentence or clause. Some examples are: *yes, no.*

> *No,* I don't think I'll join you.
> *Yes,* you did leave your gloves at the skating rink.

Comparison of Adverbs

Adverbs of manner (adverbs that tell *how*), like adjectives, can be compared upward and downward in three degrees: positive, comparative, and superlative. Adverbs can also be compared upward by two different methods.

1. Most adverbs are compared upward by using *more* for the comparative degree and *most* for the superlative degree.

Positive	Comparative	Superlative
accurately	more accurately	most accurately
happily	more happily	most happily
quickly	more quickly	most quickly

2. A few adverbs are compared upward by using *-er* for the comparative degree and *-est* for the superlative degree.

Positive	Comparative	Superlative
early	earlier	earliest
near	nearer	nearest
soon	sooner	soonest

All adverbs are compared downward by using *less* for the comparative degree and *least* for the superlative degree.

Positive	Comparative	Superlative
accurately	less accurately	least accurately
early	less early	least early
happily	less happily	least happily
quickly	less quickly	least quickly

Some adverbs are compared irregularly.

Positive	Comparative	Superlative
badly	worse	worst
far	farther	farthest
	further	furthest
little	less	least
much	more	most
well	better	best

Adverb or Adjective?

Many words that end in *-ly* are adverbs (*sharply, strongly, surely*). However, some words that end in *-ly* are adjectives (*cowardly, friendly, lovely, manly*). And some adverbs do not end in *-ly* (*far, fast, here, soon, there*). Some words can be used either as adverbs or adjectives.

Word	Adverb	Adjective
deep	Dig *deep* to find water.	We dug a *deep* well.
far	We walked *far* into the forest.	He came from a *far* country.
hard	Mark hit the ball *hard.*	It was a *hard* choice.
little, long	The world will *little* note nor *long* remember . . .	He had *little* feet and *long* legs.
near	The horse came *near.*	It was a *near* escape.
right	Turn *right* at the stop sign.	That was the *right* way to turn.
straight	He drew his lines *straight.*	He walked a *straight* line.

Other words that can be used either as adverbs or adjectives include: *close, daily, first, hard, high, late, only, tight.*

To test whether a word is an adverb or an adjective, look at how it is used in the sentence. If it modifies a noun, it is an adjective. If it modifies a verb, adjective, or other adverb, it is an adverb.

There goes Marsha on her *daily* trip to the store.
(*Daily* is an adjective modifying the noun *trip.*)

Marsha goes to the store *daily.*
(*Daily* is an adverb modifying the verb *goes.*)

Some words have two closely related adverb forms.

cheap—cheaply	near—nearly
deep—deeply	quick—quickly
hard—hardly	right—rightly
high—highly	slow—slowly
late—lately	tight—tightly

In some cases, usually in informal, short commands, the

two forms have the same meaning and can be used interchangeably.

> Go *slow* around that curve.
> Go *slowly* around that curve.

In other cases, the two forms have different meanings and cannot be used interchangeably.

> Come sit *near* me.
> You *nearly* missed that turnpike exit.

> Sam hit the ball *hard*.
> Nancy *hardly* had time to catch her breath.

Well/Good

Well can be used as both an adverb and an adjective. As an adverb, *well* means "capably or successfully."

> Richard did *well* on the math test.
> (Modifies the verb *did*)

As an adjective, *well* means "healthy" or "satisfactory."

> You look *well*.
> (Modifies the pronoun *you*)

> All is *well*.
> (Modifies the pronoun *all*)

Alert: *Good* is always an adjective and should never be used in place of *well*.

Incorrect: Margaret played *good*.
Correct: Margaret played *well*.

Bad/Badly

Badly is used only as an adverb.

> I did *badly* on my spelling test.
> (Modifies the verb *did*)

Bad is used only as an adjective.

> I feel *bad*.
> (Modifies the pronoun *I*)

Adverb Placement

Since adverbs can modify verbs, adjectives, and other adverbs, they can appear in many different sentence positions. The meaning of a sentence can vary depending on where the adverb is placed. For example:

Jack *almost* caught a dozen fish this morning.
(Twelve times, Jack came close to catching a fish.)
Jack caught *almost* a dozen fish this morning.
(Jack caught somewhat fewer than twelve fish.)

I *just* spoke with Sally.
(I spoke with Sally only a few minutes ago.)
I spoke *just* with Sally.
(Sally was the only person with whom I spoke.)

Be careful where you place adverbs such as *almost, even, hardly, just, merely, nearly, only,* and *scarcely.* Put them as close as possible to the words they modify.

Prepositions

A preposition is a word or group of words that shows the relationship of a noun or pronoun to some other word in the sentence.

The fish swam *in* the tank.
(The preposition *in* shows the relationship between the noun *tank* and the verb *swam.*)

The boy running *with* his dog slipped and fell.
(The preposition *with* shows the relationship between the noun *dog* and the participle *running.*)

Sandra hung her coat *on* the hook.
(The preposition *on* shows the relationship between the noun *hook* and the noun *coat.*)

We were talking *about* you.
(The preposition *about* shows the relationship between the pronoun *you* and the verb *were talking.*)

Here is a list of some frequently used prepositions:

about	beside	off
above	between	on
across	by	out
after	down	over
against	during	throughout
around	except	to
at	for	toward
because of	from	under
before	in	until
behind	in spite of	up
below	of	with
beneath		

Prepositional Object

The object of a preposition is the noun or pronoun that follows a preposition which shows the object's relationship to another word.

What do you think *about* his *idea?*
(The noun *idea* is the object of the preposition *about.*)

Harold loves hamburgers broiled *on* the *grill.*
(The noun *grill* is the object of the preposition *on.*)

Come sit *beside me.*
(The pronoun *me* is the object of the preposition *beside.*)

Preposition or Adverb?

Many words that act as prepositions can also act as adverbs. For example:

The cat ran *out* the door.
(Out acts as a preposition, taking the object *door.)*

The cat ran *out.*
(Out acts as an adverb, modifying the verb *ran.)*

We stumbled *down* the hill.
(Down acts as a preposition, taking the object *hill.)*

We stumbled *down*.
(Down acts as an adverb, modifying the verb stumbled.)

The smoke drifted *up* the chimney.
(Up acts as a preposition, taking the object chimney.)

The smoke drifted *up*.
(Up acts as an adverb, modifying the verb drifted.)

To tell whether the word acts as a preposition or an adverb, see if it takes an object. If it does, it acts as a preposition. If not, it acts as an adverb.

Which Prepositions to Use?

Some nouns, adjectives, and verbs take the same preposition all or most of the time.

account for	foreign to	sensitive to
argue with	happy about	similar to
capable of	independent of	sympathize with
confide in	inseparable from	tamper with
desirous of	obedient to	
envious of	protest against	

But some words routinely take several different prepositions, depending on meaning:

angry at	concerned for	quarrel over
angry with	concerned with	quarrel with
apply for	free from	speak against
apply to	free of	speak until
careless about	part from	worried by
careless of	part with	worried throughout

The main word entry in a good dictionary will explain the changes in meaning that different prepositions bring about. If you are unsure of which preposition to use, always consult your dictionary.

Which Prepositions to Leave Out?

An object can have more than one preposition.

> Charlie was interested *in* and curious *about* local *politics.*

In this example, *interested* takes the preposition *in. Curious* takes the preposition *about.* Both prepositions must appear in the sentence.
> Here's a different example:

> Charlie was interested and involved *in* local politics.

Here, both *interested* and *involved* take the preposition *in.* To repeat the preposition would make the sentence unnecessarily wordy. Use the preposition *in* only once.

Between/Among

Use *between* for two persons or items.

> John interrupted a private discussion *between Patty* and *me.*

Use *among* for three or more persons or items.

> The guitar players strolled *among* the *diners* in the Spanish restaurant.

Ending Sentences with Prepositions

Often when speaking, we end sentences with prepositions.

> Whom is she waiting *for?*
> Whom is Tom going *with?*

Some people object to this form for writing, and prefer

> *For* whom is she waiting?
> *With* whom is Tom going?

Find out, and follow, the style your teacher prefers.

Conjunctions

A conjunction joins words, phrases, clauses, or sentences.

There are three kinds of conjunctions: coordinating, subordinating, and correlative.

Coordinating Conjunctions

Coordinating conjunctions join grammatically equal structures: words with words; phrases with phrases; clauses with clauses; and sentences with sentences. The most common coordinating conjunctions are *and, but, for, or, nor, so,* and *yet.*

> **Words with words**: Samantha will play basketball *or* baseball.
> (The coordinating conjunction *or* joins the two nouns *basketball* and *baseball.*)
>
> **Phrases with phrases**: On the bench, Andy sat strumming his guitar *and* humming a tune.
> (The coordinating conjunction *and* joins the two participial phrases *strumming his guitar* and *humming a tune.*)
>
> **Subordinate clauses with subordinate clauses**: That is the woman who works in the bakery *but* who hates sweets.
> (The coordinating conjunction *but* joins the two subordinate clauses *who works in the bakery* and *who hates sweets.*)
>
> **Sentences with sentences**: Our team members vowed to win the trophy. *Yet* they failed.
> (The coordinating conjunction *yet* links the two complete thoughts, *Our team members vowed to win the trophy* and *they failed.*)

Subordinating Conjunctions

Subordinating conjunctions connect subordinate clauses to main clauses. The most common subordinating conjunctions include:

after	before	so that	when
although	how	that	where
as	if	though	while
as if	in order that	till	why
because	since	unless	

We will meet for practice on the field tomorrow *unless* it rains. (The subordinating conjunction *unless* connects the subordinate clause, *unless it rains,* to the main clause.)

You must finish your homework *if* you wish to go out. (The subordinating conjunction *if* connects the subordinate clause, *if you wish to go out,* to the main clause.)

Correlative Conjunctions

Correlative conjunctions are word pairs used as conjunctions. Some common correlative conjunctions are:

both . . . and	not only . . . but (also)
either . . . or	whether . . . or
neither . . . nor	

Marsha had *neither* the time *nor* the patience to listen to Judy's complaints.

We couldn't decide *whether* to stay *or* to go.

Placing Correlative Conjunctions

Place correlative conjunctions so that they clearly join the words you wish to connect.

Unclear: Mark *both* likes Monica *and* Sandy.
Clear: Mark likes *both* Monica *and* Sandy.

Unclear: Randy *not only* got A's in math *but* in English.
Clear: Randy got A's *not only* in math *but* in English.

Words Correlative Conjunctions Join

Correlative conjunctions join similar sentence parts—nouns with nouns, adjectives with adjectives, prepositional phrases with prepositional phrases, for example.

> **Incorrect:** Rita is both *talented* and *makes friends easily.*
> **Correct:** Rita is both *talented* and *likable.*

Talented and *likable* are both predicate adjectives. *Makes friends easily* is a predicate.

> **Incorrect:** We went not only *to the bank* but also *to eat lunch.*
> **Correct:** We went not only *to the bank* but also *to the cafe for lunch.*

To the bank and *to the cafe for lunch* are prepositional phrases. *To eat lunch* is an infinitive phrase.

Interjections

An interjection is a word or phrase that shows emotion.

Interjections have no grammatical connection with the other words in a sentence. Interjections that show strong emotion take an exclamation point. Those that show mild emotion take a comma. Common interjections include: *bravo, hurrah, oh, ouch,* and *whoops.*

> *Oh,* never mind.
> *Ouch!* That hurt.
> *Hey!* You almost drove through a stop sign.

Alert: We use interjections more in speaking than writing. Too many interjections make writing dull, not exciting. When you write, avoid the "excitement" of this paragraph:

Oh, no! I can't believe it! Not again! This is the third time they've tried! You mean they still can't pass the driving test! That's terrible! I'm glad I passed mine!

II SENTENCE-BUILDING GUIDELINES

Putting words together to form effective sentences is the subject of this section.

Subject

Noun

Verb

Clause

Sentence-Building Guidelines

S entences are important to good communication. They are extremely flexible and interesting to work with. Sentences always have two basic parts: a subject and predicate. But you can arrange these in countless ways to make your point. You can communicate almost anything once you learn how to build good sentences. This section will help you learn how.

Complete Sentences

Complete sentences are groups of related words that always have a subject and predicate, and always state a complete thought.

Subject

The subject of a sentence is what or whom you are talking about.

> *I* know. (subject = *I*)
>
> *The bright summer sun* glimmered through the trees. (subject = *The bright summer sun*)
>
> *My friend Sandra* went to the movies. (subject = *My friend Sandra*)

Simple and Complete Subjects

There are several ways of describing a sentence's subject. The simple subject is the noun or pronoun you are talking about. The complete subject is the simple subject plus all the words that go with it.

> *The bright summer sun* glimmered through the trees. (simple subject = *sun*) (complete subject = *The bright summer sun*)

My friend Sandra went to the movies.
(simple subject = *Sandra*)
(complete subject = *My friend Sandra*)

The newly opened soda bubbled.
(simple subject = *soda*)
(complete subject = *The newly opened soda*)

In sentences where there is only one noun or pronoun in the subject, that word is the simple and complete subject.

I know. (simple and complete subject = *I*)

Simple and Compound Subjects

We also say a sentence has a simple subject when there is only one noun or pronoun as the subject. A sentence has a compound subject when there are two or more nouns or pronouns as the subject.

I know. (simple subject = *I*)

She and I know. (compound subject = *she and I*)

My friend *Sandra* went to the movies.
(simple subject = *Sandra*)

My friends *Sandra and Jim* went to the movies.
(compound subject = *Sandra and Jim*)

Cathy campaigned for the class president.
(simple subject = *Cathy*)

Cathy, Max, and I campaigned for the class president.
(compound subject = *Cathy, Max, and I*)

Predicate

The predicate is the part of a sentence that says something about the subject.

She and I *know*. (predicate = *know*)

The bright summer sun *glimmered through the trees.*
(predicate = *glimmered through the trees*)

My friends Sandra and Jim *went to the movies.*
(predicate = *went to the movies*)

The newly opened soda *bubbled.*
(predicate = *bubbled*)

Cathy, Max, and I *campaigned for the class president.*
(predicate = *campaigned for the class president*)

Simple and Complete Predicates

There are several ways of describing a sentence's predicate. The simple predicate is the verb that says something about the subject. The complete predicate is the verb and all the words that go with it.

The bright summer sun *glimmered through the trees.*
(simple predicate = *glimmered*)
(complete predicate = *glimmered through the trees*)

My friends Sandra and Jim *went to the movies.*
(simple predicate = *went*)
(complete predicate = *went to the movies*)

Cathy, Max, and I *campaigned for the class president.*
(simple predicate = *campaigned*)
(complete predicate = *campaigned for the class president*)

In sentences where there is only one verb in the predicate, that word is the simple and complete predicate.

She and I *know.* (simple and complete predicate = *know*)
The newly opened soda *bubbled.*
(simple and complete predicate = *bubbled*)

Simple and Compound Predicates

We also say a sentence has a simple predicate when there is only one verb for the subject. A compound predicate has two or more verbs for the same subject or subjects.

The newly opened soda *bubbled.*
(simple predicate = *bubbled*)

The newly opened soda *bubbled and fizzed.*
(compound predicate = *bubbled and fizzed*)

Cathy, Max, and I *campaigned* for the class president.
(simple predicate = *campaigned*)

Cathy, Max, and I *campaigned and voted* for the class president. (compound predicate = *campaigned and voted*)

Richard *danced* in the school play.
(simple predicate = *danced*)

Richard *danced and sang* in the school play.
(compound predicate = *danced and sang*)

Alert: When teachers talk about a sentence's subject or predicate, they usually mean the simple subject or predicate. Ask if you are unsure.

Subject/Predicate Order

Most often, the subject comes before the predicate.

The *kite* / *flew* up and away. (subject = *kite;* verb = *flew*)
The *letter* / *was* in the mailbox.
(subject = *letter;* verb = *was*)

To make a sentence more interesting, you may reorganize the predicate and put it first.

Up and away *flew* / the *kite.*
In the mailbox *was* / the *letter.*

Complete Thoughts and Fragments

A complete sentence is always a complete thought. Incomplete thoughts are called fragments.

The cheerful little girl (fragment)
The cheerful little girl played baseball in the park. (complete thought)

Reflected the sunlight (fragment)
The glass skyscraper reflected the sunlight. (complete thought)

Sticky black mud covered sidewalk (fragment)
The sticky black mud covered the sidewalk. (complete thought)

When I graduate (fragment)
When I graduate, I'm joining VISTA. (complete thought)

Requests and Commands

Can you find the subject in these sentences?

> Please finish your dinner.
> Work a little longer.
> Keep quiet!

The first sentence is a request. The second is a mild command. The third is a strong command. All have the understood subject *you*. They are complete thoughts, with a subject and verb, even though *you* doesn't show. They are therefore all complete sentences.

Phrases

Phrases are groups of two or more related words that add information to different sentence parts. Many phrases have predicates, but they do not have subjects and predicates, as sentences and clauses do. There are four types of phrases: prepositional, participial, gerund, and infinitive phrases.

Prepositional Phrases

Prepositional phrases consist of a preposition, its object, and any modifiers. Prepositional phrases are always used as adjectives or adverbs.

> by the sunny garden
> after my arrival
> near the cool fountain
> around the window
> with the gray suit
> in good shape

Here are examples of prepositional phrases used in sentences.

> Did you see the lights *around the window?*
> (acts as an adjective; modifies *lights*)

> The man *with the gray suit* is my father.
> (acts as an adjective; modifies *man*)

The wrestlers kept *in good shape.*
(acts as an adverb, modifies *kept*)

You will often find prepositional phrases in other types of phrases. Some examples follow.

Participial Phrases

Participial phrases consist of a past or present participle, its object, and any modifiers. (Past participles are verbs usually ending in *-ed.* Present participles are verbs always ending in *-ing.*) Participial phrases are used only as adjectives.

> worried sick
> surprised at the news
> locked from within
> setting the lights around the window
> wearing the gray suit
> keeping in good shape

Here are examples of participial phrases used in sentences:

> Did you see them *setting the lights around the window?*
> (acts as an adjective; modifies *them*)

> The man *wearing the gray suit* is my father.
> (acts as an adjective; modifies *man*)

> The wrestlers, *keeping in good shape,* worked out.
> (acts as an adjective; modifies *wrestlers*)

Gerund Phrases

Gerund phrases consist of a gerund (present participle, ending in *-ing*), its objects, and any modifiers. Gerunds and present participles look exactly alike. The difference between gerund phrases and participial phrases is how you use them in sentences. Gerund phrases are always used as nouns. Participial phrases are always used as adjectives.

These sentences have the same phrases as the previous examples. But here, the phrases are used as nouns. The phrases are therefore gerund phrases.

> *Setting the lights around the window* was a wonderful idea.
> (acts as a noun; used as the subject of the sentence)

My father likes *wearing the gray suit.*
(acts as a noun; used as a direct object)

Their goal, *keeping in good shape,* was important to the wrestlers.
(acts as a noun; used as an appositive for *goal*)

Alert: Do not confuse gerund phrases with participial phrases. Gerund phrases are used as nouns. Participial phrases are used as adjectives.

Swimming laps takes stamina. (gerund phrase, acting as a noun; subject of the sentence.)
The girl *swimming laps* is my sister. (participial phrase, acting as an adjective; modifies the noun *girl*)

Infinitive Phrases

Infinitive phrases consist of an infinitive, its objects, and any modifiers. Infinitive phrases are used as nouns, adjectives, and adverbs.

to go inside
to become a pilot
to drive safely
to set the lights around the window
to wear the gray suit
to keep in good shape

Here are some examples of infinitive phrases used in sentences.

The idea *to set the lights around the window* was wonderful. (acts as an adjective; modifies *idea*)

My father likes *to wear the gray suit.*
(acts as a noun; used as a direct object)

The wrestlers worked out *to keep in good shape.*
(acts as an adverb; modifies the verb *worked*)

Misplaced Modifiers

When you put modifiers in the wrong places, confusing, absurd, or silly statements can result. Here are some sentences with misplaced modifiers. Notice that there can be more than one way to correct these errors.

Incorrect: Turn on the switch *for beginners.*

(There's no special switch for beginners. But someone might begin by turning on a switch. This prepositional phrase is in the wrong place.)

Correct: *For beginners,* turn on the switch.

Correct: The first step is turning on the switch.

Incorrect: Martin grabbed for the books feeling frustrated.

(Martin, not the books, felt frustrated. This participial phrase is in the wrong place.)

Correct: Martin, *feeling frustrated,* grabbed for the books.

Correct: A frustrated Martin grabbed for the books.

Incorrect: Shelley needs her coat to keep warm outside.

(Shelley doesn't care if her coat keeps warm outside. Shelley needs to keep herself warm. This infinitive phrase is in the wrong place.)

Correct: Shelley, *to keep warm outside,* needs her coat.

Correct: *To keep warm outside,* Shelley needs her coat.

Clauses

Clauses are groups of related words that have both a subject and predicate. Clauses can be classified a number of ways.

Independent Clauses

Independent, or main, clauses can stand by themselves. They express complete thoughts. Independent clauses can be long or short.

Rain falls

Roses are red

> Twenty persons attended the ceremony
> The Spanish class visited a Mexican restaurant.
> The passenger in the brown hat who is talking to the train conductor seems furious about the delay

Adding periods to independent clauses makes them complete sentences. For example:

> Rain falls.
> Roses are red.
> Twenty persons attended the ceremony.

Dependent Clauses

Clauses that cannot stand by themselves are called dependent, or subordinate, clauses. They are incomplete thoughts, or fragments. Dependent clauses need independent clauses to complete their meaning. Dependent clauses act as adjectives, adverbs, or nouns.

Adjective Clauses. Adjective clauses can modify any noun or pronoun. They can be used in several ways.

To modify a subject:

> The package *that Sue wrapped* was the prettiest.
> (modifies *package*)

To modify a predicate nominative:

> The tall fire fighter is the one *who saved my cat.*
> (modifies *one*)

To modify a direct object:

> The puppy chased the stick *that its owner threw.*
> (modifies *stick*)

To modify an indirect object:

> We sent our classmate *who was sick* a get-well card.
> (modifies *classmate*)

To modify a prepositional object:

> We walked up the hill *where the hut stood.*
> (modifies *hill*)

Adverb Clauses. Adverb clauses can modify any verb, adjective, or adverb. They can be used in several ways.

To modify a verb:

> We ate *when the guests arrived.*
> (modifies *ate*)

To modify an adjective:

> I baked enough cupcakes *so that there is one for each child.*
> (modifies *enough*)

To modify an adverb:

> The stereo was so loud *that I couldn't hear the phone.*
> (modifies *so*)

To modify a predicate adjective:

> Rachel is often cranky *when she first wakes up.*
> (modifies *cranky*)

Noun Clauses. Noun clauses can take the place of any noun or pronoun. They can be used in several ways.

As a subject:

> *What happened at the party* surprised everyone.
> (subject of the verb *surprised*)

As a direct object:

> Sara knew *that her outfit was attractive.*
> (object of the verb *knew*)

As an indirect object:

> We will give *whoever wants one* a copy of the entire speech.
> (indirect object of the verb *give*)

As a prepositional object:

> The campers took nothing except *what they could carry in their packs.* (object of the preposition *except*)

As a predicate nominative:

> The question is *whether we should build a house or buy one.* (predicate nominative after the linking verb *is*)

As an appositive:

> His first thought, *that a pipe had burst,* was incorrect. (appositive for the noun *thought*)

Elliptical Clauses

All clauses contain a subject and predicate. But these aren't always written out completely. When part of a clause is understood rather than written, the clause is an elliptical clause. Elliptical clauses make sentences less wordy, and they add variety to speaking and writing.

> Ms. Jones retired from the mill in November; *Mr. Jones, a month later.* (a complete independent clause followed by an elliptical independent clause)

Completely written out, this sentence would read:

> Ms. Jones retired from the mill in November; Mr. Jones *retired from the mill* a month later. (two complete independent clauses)

The verb and a prepositional phrase, *retired from the mill,* are missing in the elliptical clause in the first example. A comma has taken their place, as is often the case in elliptical constructions.

> *While listening to the radio,* Sam heard an interview with the Senator. (an elliptical dependent clause followed by a complete independent clause)

Completely written out, this sentence would read:

> While *he was* listening to the radio, Sam heard an interview with the Senator. (a complete dependent clause followed by a complete independent clause)

The subject, *he,* and part of the verb, *was,* are missing in the elliptical clause in the first example.

Restrictive and Nonrestrictive Clauses

Clauses are either restrictive or nonrestrictive. Restrictive clauses are necessary sentence parts. They identify people and things. Removing them from sentences would alter the sentences' meanings. The relative pronoun *that* introduces restrictive clauses.

Nonrestrictive clauses give additional information about persons or things. You can omit nonrestrictive clauses from sentences without changing their meanings. The relative pronouns *who* or *which* often introduce nonrestrictive clauses. Commas set them off.

Restrictive: The tapes *that we can't find* might be in Dad's car.

Nonrestrictive: The tapes, *which are my favorites*, might be in Dad's car.

Restrictive: The meal *that I liked best* came with hot fudge sundaes for dessert.

Nonrestrictive: The meal, *which was my first all day,* came with hot fudge sundaes for dessert.

Restrictive: The girl *sitting by me* was my sister.

Nonrestrictive: My sister, *sitting by me,* slowly ate her ice cream.

Sentence Structure

Sentences can be classified in several ways. One is by their structure. The four kinds of sentence structure are: simple, compound, complex, and compound-complex.

Simple Sentences

Simple sentences are made up of one independent (main) clause. A simple sentence can have a simple subject and predicate, a compound subject or predicate, or both a compound subject and a compound predicate.

The *boy* / *ate* the apple. (simple subject and predicate)

A *man* and his *son* / *came* to the store. (compound subject and simple predicate)

The *pianist* / *bowed* to the audience and *sat down* at the piano. (simple subject and compound predicate)

My *brother* and *sister* / *swim* and *ski*. (compound subject and compound predicate)

Compound Sentences

Compound sentences have two or more related but independent clauses. The clauses are connected by semicolons; coordinating conjunctions like *and, but,* or *so;* and semicolons followed by conjunctive adverbs like *however, nevertheless,* and *therefore.*

> We don't like horror movies; we left the theater immediately.
>
> We don't like horror movies *and* we left the theater immediately.
>
> We don't like horror movies; *therefore,* we left the theater immediately.

Complex Sentences

Complex sentences have one independent clause and one or more dependent clauses.

> dependent clause   independent clause
> Although Harry was late, we let him join the game.
>
> dependent clause   independent clause
> After I finished my homework, I went to the store
>
> dependent clause
> that you told me about.

Compound-Complex Sentences

Compound-complex sentences have two or more independent clauses and one or more dependent clauses.

> dependent clause   independent clause
> When the house gets cold in winter, Father lights a fire in
>
> independent clause
> the fireplace and Mother makes some hot chocolate.

dependent clause   independent clause

If Sally can come to visit tomorrow, we'll go to the park;

dependent clause   independent clause

if she can't, I'll stay home and read.

Sentence Types

You can classify sentences according to what they do. The four sentence types are: declarative, interrogative, imperative, and exclamatory.

Declarative Sentences

Sentences that state facts or make assertions are declarative sentences. Declarative sentences end with a period. Most sentences are declarative sentences.

> The boy is tall.
> The new factory provided jobs for much of the community.
> The blouse's tag scratched the back of Kim's neck when she
> moved.

Interrogative Sentences

Sentences that ask questions are interrogative sentences. Interrogative sentences end with a question mark.

> Is there a shorter route to the mall?
> What time is it?
> Do you like Oriental food?

Rhetorical questions end with exclamation points rather than question marks. These questions are more like exclamations than questions. No answer is expected.

> Why did I ever do that!
> How can anyone "forget" to go to school!

Imperative Sentences

Sentences that give commands or make requests are imperative sentences. *You* is the understood subject of imperative sentences.

Mild commands end with a period. Strong commands end with an exclamation point. Requests end with a period.

> Bring the paper with you when you come in. (mild command)
> Go away! (strong command)
> Please take out the garbage. (request)

Exclamatory Sentences

Sentences that show strong feeling are exclamatory sentences. They end with exclamation points.

> You should be ashamed of yourself!
> I can't stand this any more!

Sentence Arrangement

You can classify sentences according to how you arrange their words.

Loose Sentences

Loose sentences present a complete thought first and then add details to strengthen it.

> The new team was a strong one with a combination of enthusiastic rookies and seasoned athletes.
> The spy plunged into the rapids, seeking to escape from the counteragents.

Loose sentences are direct and easy to follow. They help the reader grasp the main thought quickly. But too many loose sentences used together can be boring.

Periodic Sentences

Periodic sentences place the main thought last.

> With a combination of enthusiastic rookies and seasoned athletes, the new team was a strong one.
>
> Seeking to escape from the counteragents, the spy plunged into the rapids.

Periodic sentences provide variety and often create a sense of drama by keeping the main thought until the end. When you use loose and periodic sentences together, your writing is more interesting and exciting.

Balanced Sentences

Balanced sentences use the same or similar word forms more than once to present thoughts for comparison or contrast.

> Silently permitting defeat is harder than actively fighting defeat.
>
> To learn is difficult, to know a joy.

Balanced sentences have a definite pattern. Used occasionally, they have a dramatic effect.

Alert: You have already seen these two sentences:

Ms. Jones retired from the mill in November; Mr. Jones, a month later.

To learn is difficult, to know a joy.

The second clause in both cases is elliptical (incomplete). In the first example, a semicolon introduces the elliptical clause and a comma replaces the missing words *retired from the mill*. In the second example, a comma introduces the elliptical clause and no punctuation replaces the missing word *is*.

Depending on length, you can use either type of punctuation (none for *is* in the second example). Usually, the longer the sentence, the more you need to use the first type.

Repetition and Wordiness

Repetitious and wordy (or redundant) sentences are weak. Repetition means using the same words or thoughts more than once. Wordy means using too many words to say what you mean.

When you build sentences, get to the point. Don't go around it. Here are examples of repetitious and wordy sentences, with ways to improve them:

Weak: A large, big, huge ship sailed into the harbor.

Better: An enormous ship sailed into the harbor.

Weak: The tiny, small, petite poodle sat on the woman's lap.

Better: The teeny poodle sat on the woman's lap.

Weak: The dining room table, hallway table, and kitchen table were all covered with French lace.

Better: French lace covered the dining room, hallway, and kitchen tables.

Weak: The scissors could possibly be located in the drawer, in the cupboard, or in the sewing basket.

Better: The scissors might be in the drawer, cupboard, or sewing basket.

Weak: There were seven persons who attended.

Better: Seven persons attended.

Weak: No one came with the exception of Jane.

Better: Only Jane came.

Weak: I cannot find the time to talk to you now.

Better: I cannot talk now.

Weak: It is a good idea to inspect your house for termites every now and then.

Better: A good idea is to inspect your house for termites occasionally.

Weak: I regret very much that I have to inform you that the decision is final.

Better: Unfortunately, the decision is final.

Weak: I only met him on one occasion.
Better: I met him once.

Weak: It snows in April once in a great while.
Better: It rarely snows in April.

Weak: Father is of the belief that practice makes perfect.
Better: Father believes practice makes perfect.

Weak: The clown was funny. Everyone laughed at the clown. Dimsey was the name of the character who brought so much laughter. Dimsey played tricks and told jokes to make the crowd laugh. The clown did many humorous things.
Better: A clown named Dimsey was the crowd's favorite. His actions, tricks, and jokes were hilarious.

I CAPITALIZATION AND PUNCTUATION GUIDELINES

This section contains thirty-one guidelines for proper capitalization. It also describes how to use punctuation marks.

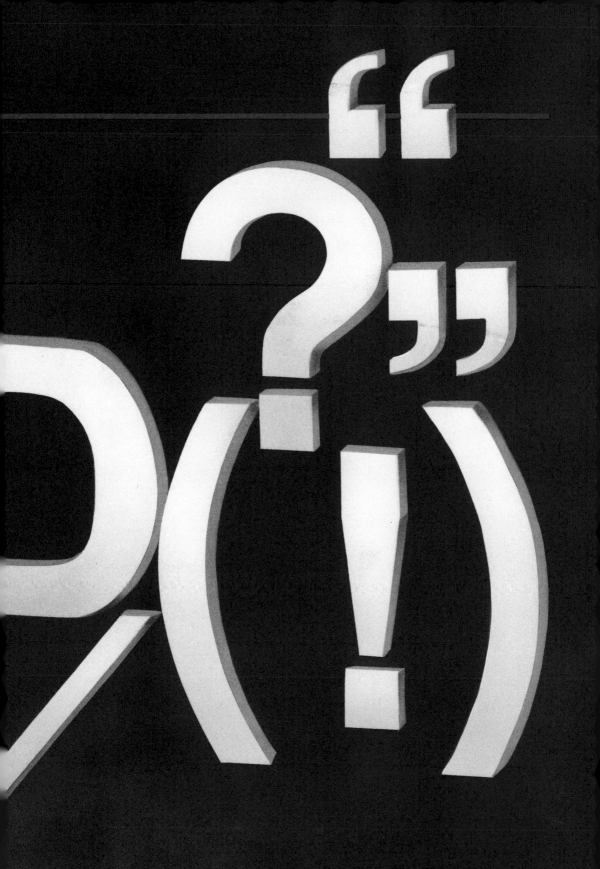

Capitalization and Punctuation Guidelines

*C*apital letters are signals to readers. They announce new sentences, people's names, and book titles. They show the beginning of direct quotations and professional titles. Punctuation has one purpose: to make writing clear and effective. This section gives useful guidelines to follow for capitalization and punctuation.

Capitalization Guidelines

Knowing when to use capital and lower-case letters can sometimes be confusing. This list gives you some general capitalization rules to follow.

1. Capitalize proper nouns.

James Smith	America	Shakespeare	Zeus

2. Capitalize proper adjectives. Proper adjectives are adjectives that are formed from proper nouns and proper nouns that are used as adjectives.

American tourist	Shakespearean play	Chinese art
Iowa farmers	New England states	Texas chili

Lower-case the words in the following list. Even though they come from proper nouns, they are so commonly used that they are not capitalized.

chinaware	pasteurized milk
derby hat	scotch plaid
frankfurter (hot dog)	vienna bread
manila envelope	

3. Capitalize the pronoun *I* and the interjection *O*.

Rejoice, O ye people, for I bring you glad tidings.

4. Capitalize words that show family relationship when they are used instead or as part of a name.

>I asked Mother if Uncle John was coming.

Lower-case these words when a possessive such as *my, your,* or *their* comes before them.

>My mother visited her uncle.

5. Capitalize nicknames and other identifying names.

>Babe Ruth   Great Emancipator   Richard the Lion-Hearted

6. Capitalize professional titles when they come immediately before a personal name.

>General Patton   Pope John Paul II   President de Gaulle

Lower-case professional titles that don't come before a name.

>George S. Patton was a great American general.
>Charles de Gaulle, president of France

7. Capitalize academic titles and their abbreviations when they follow a personal name.

>Jane Doe, Doctor of Philosophy   John Smith, M.D.
>Maria Ames, R.N.

8. Capitalize personified nouns.

>none of Beauty's daughters

9. Capitalize brand names.

>Comet (cleanser)   Cougar (car)   Rice Krispies

10. Capitalize specific political and geographical locations (and the adjectives that come from them).

>Chicago   Dade County   Asia   Asian

11. Capitalize the names of all nationalities, races, and tribes (and the adjectives that come from them).

>German   Japanese   Caucasian   Sioux

12. Capitalize direction words used to show a specific place.

>North Pole   Far East   Midwest   the South

Lower-case *north, south, east,* and *west* when they refer to a direction or a section of a state.

> We live west of Washington and vacation in northern Virginia.

13. Capitalize the names of specific geographic features and the common nouns that are part of the proper names.

> Mississippi River   Niagara Falls   Pacific Ocean

But:

> Mississippi and Ohio rivers   falls of the Niagara

14. Capitalize the names of buildings, monuments, streets, bridges, parks, and other specific locations, and the common nouns that are part of the proper names.

> White House   Statue of Liberty   Fifth Avenue
> U.S. Route 34   Brooklyn Bridge   Grant Park

15. Capitalize the names of organizations, businesses, and institutions.

> League of Women Voters   General Foods Corporation
> Baylor University   Burnsville Junior
> High School

16. Capitalize the names of political parties and religious denominations and their members.

> Democratic Party   Democrat
> Islam   Moslem

17. Capitalize the names of sacred writings and of specific creeds, confessions of faith, and prayers.

> Bible   Talmud   Koran
> Apostles' Creed   Hail Mary   Lord's Prayer

18. Capitalize nouns and pronouns that refer to a specific Supreme Being.

> God   Allah   Jehovah   Lord
> Trust in Him for He is good.

But:

> The Romans believed in many gods.

19. Capitalize specific cultural and historical events, wars, treaties, laws, and documents.

> American Revolution   World War II
> Homestead Act   Articles of Confederation

20. Capitalize the names of historical and cultural periods.

> Middle Ages   Roaring Twenties   Era of Good Feeling

But:

> colonial period   twentieth century   postwar era

21. Capitalize the names of specific branches, departments, and other divisions of government.

> Senate   Department of State
> Los Angeles   Library of Congress
>   Park District

But:

> state legislature   traffic court   public library

22. Capitalize the names of specific awards and prizes.

> Nobel Peace Prize   Academy Award   Medal of Honor

23. Capitalize the names of specific trains, planes, ships, satellites, and submarines. (These specific names are also italicized or underlined.)

> *Orient Express*   *Spirit of St. Louis*
> *Lusitania*   *Sputnik*

24. Capitalize the names of stars, constellations, planets, and other astronomical designations.

> North Star   Big Dipper   Milky Way
> planets Earth and Venus

But:

> moon   earth's circumference
> sun   Halley's comet

25. Capitalize the days of the week, months of the year, and holidays. Lower-case the seasons.

> Tuesday   October   Memorial Day   Fourth of July
> spring   fall   summer   winter

26. Capitalize the first word of a sentence or a word or phrase that has the force of a sentence.

> The children are running across the street.
> Stop!   Wow!

27. Capitalize the first word of a direct quotation.

> "We're leaving tomorrow," said Mary.
> Jane replied, "Have a good trip."

28. Capitalize the first word of a complete statement following a colon (:).

> Here is my decision: You will not go to the concert.

29. Capitalize the first word in a letter's greeting or close.

> Gentlemen: Dear Sir: My dear Ellen:
> Yours truly,   Sincerely yours,   With love,

30. In titles of works of art, books, magazines, newspapers, poems, songs, plays, articles, television shows, reports, and other writing, capitalize the first and last words and all other words except articles, coordinate conjunctions, and prepositions. If five letters long or more, prepositions may be capitalized.

> *Mona Lisa*   *Up the Down Staircase*
> *The Saturday Evening Post*
> "Come In"   "Fire and Rain"   *A Chorus Line*
> "Learning About Atoms"

31. Capitalize the parts of a book when reference is made from one part to another of the same book.

> This information is in Chapter 1.

But:

> This chapter ends the book.

Punctuation Guidelines

This list presents the punctuation marks and their most common uses.

A Period (.) Is Used—

1. At the end of complete sentences, including requests and mild commands.

> The sun was shining.
> Please wash the car.
> Come early.

2. After each number or letter that begins an outline heading.

> WHY I LIKE SPORTS
> I. Improves my health
>   A. Indoor exercise
>   1. Weight training

3. After initials and many abbreviations, especially if the abbreviation spells a word.

> J. R. R. Tolkien   in.   ft.   Ms.   Dr.   U.S.   C.O.D.

The abbreviations for some organizations and government agencies use no periods.

> FBI   VISTA   ABC   IBM

A Question Mark (?) Is Used—

At the end of direct questions, statements ending with a question, or words or sentences that ask a question.

> Why did you buy that dress?   That was silly, wasn't it?
> Why?   You're leaving now?

An Exclamation Point (!) Is Used—

1. After a word, phrase, or sentence that expresses strong feeling.

> Yuch!   What a beautiful day!   This puzzle is impossible!

2. To strengthen statements or commands.

> Okay, I'll forget about it!
> I'm supposed to take three tests in one day!
> Go away!

3. After a rhetorical question.

> Who says so!

A Colon (:) Is Used—

1. After a complete sentence followed by a list.

> Students carry many things: books, notebooks, and brown-bag lunches.

2. After a statement followed by a clause that further explains the statement.

> Today's mothers often find themselves with a double workload: They have jobs and housework.

3. After a formal letter's greeting.

> Dear Sir or Madam: Dear Ms. Williams:

4. To separate hours from minutes, parts of a named source, or parts of a book title.

> 6:30 A.M.   Genesis 1:15   *Cleopatra: Sister of the Moon*

A Comma (,) Is Used—

1. To separate long coordinate clauses of a compound sentence.

> She could go home now, but she would rather wait for her friend.

But:

> She said no and that's that.

2. Between words, phrases, or clauses in a series.

> Jane carried her coat, hat, and gloves.
> Did they meet at school, in church, or at a party?
> I washed the dishes, Joe dried them, and Sam put them away.

3. To set off phrases and dependent clauses that come before the main clause of a sentence.

> By taking the tollway, Dad saved fifteen minutes.
> Although we were tired, we continued to study.

4. To set off phrases, clauses, or appositives that are not required for a sentence to have meaning.

> The nurses, kind as they were, couldn't replace Mother.
> Mr. Garcia, the principal, is well organized.

5. To set off coordinate phrases modifying the same noun.

> Her hair is as long as, but darker than, mine.

6. Between sentence parts that show contrast or comparison.

> The more time you take now, the less you'll have later.

7. To stand for one or more missing words.

> The eggs were runny; the bacon, greasy; and the toast, burnt.

8. Often, to separate short elliptical clauses from complete independent clauses.

> To err is human, to forgive divine.

9. To separate identical or similar words.

> Walk in, in groups of three.
> They put theirs, there.

10. To separate words that might be mistakenly joined when reading a sentence.

> Soon after, the pool closed for repairs.

11. To set off words that introduce a sentence (*first, second, yes, no, oh*) or suggest a break in thought (*however, namely, of course*).

> First, write down your name.   No, I can't do that.
> The car broke down, of course, before we got to school.

12. To set off the name of a person spoken to.

> Kevin, your bicycle is across the street.
> Your grades, Mary, are improving.

13. To set off a short quotation from the rest of the sentence.

> "I'll order the drapes today," Mother said.
> "I wish," John whispered, "that this class would end."

14. After an informal letter's greeting and close.

> Dear Mom and Dad,   Sincerely yours,   With love,

15. Before any full or abbreviated title that follows a person's name.

> Janet Brown, Dean of Students   J. E. Lopez, M.D.

16. To separate the parts of a date, an address (except zip code), or a geographic location.

> May 31, 1969   Christmas Day, 1976
> We lived at 5615 Martin Drive, Lima, Ohio 45809.
> Disneyland is in Anaheim, California.

17. To set off groups of thousands in large numbers.

> 1,000   42,536   103,789,450

18. To separate unrelated numbers in a sentence.

> In 1986, 400 students graduated from our school.

A Semicolon (;) Is Used—

1. Between parts of a compound sentence when they are not joined by the conjunctions *and, but, for, nor,* or *or.*

> I want to finish this report now; I'll watch TV later.

2. To separate independent clauses when they are long or already have commas elsewhere.

> I bought hot dogs, onions, and relish; but I forgot the buns, mustard, and peppers.
> John took French this year; Gale, German and art.

3. After each clause in a series of three or more clauses.

> Lightning flashed nearby; the thunder roared above our heads; and we called off the game on account of rain.

If the clauses in the series are short, you may use commas.

> Lightning flashed, thunder roared, and down came the rain.

4. To separate items in a series when commas are needed elsewhere.

> Attending the meeting were Mr. Sloan, the adviser; Mrs. Bates, the speaker; and Mr. Green, the principal.

5. Before words like *hence, however, nevertheless, therefore,* and *thus* when they connect two independent clauses.

> Today is a holiday; *therefore*, we can go to the show.

6. Before expressions that explain, such as *for example, for instance, that is,* and *namely,* when a stronger break than a comma is needed.

> Teen-agers like to have their own phones for two reasons; namely, privacy and convenience.

A Dash (—) Is Used—

1. To show a sudden change in thought.

> The best way to finish that—but no, you don't want my opinion.

2. To suggest halting or hesitating speech.

> "I—er—ah—can't seem to find it," she mumbled.

3. Before a repeated word or expression.

> He was tired—tired of weeding the lawn.

4. To emphasize or define a part of a sentence.

> Marge Smith—the player from Iowa—won the match.

5. Before a summary introduced by words like *all* or *this.*

> Katie, Tony, and Jay—all these students got perfect scores.

To make a dash, use one line (—) when writing by hand. When typing, use two hyphens (--).

An Apostrophe (') Is Used—

1. To form noun possessives.

Singular possessive	Plural possessive
the tree's leaves	the trees' leaves
Mary's house	the Johnsons' house
Charles's mother	Tom and Charles's mother (But: Tom's and Charles's mothers)

2. To show one or more missing letters, words, or numbers.

>   can't (cannot)   one o'clock (one of the clock)
>   '86 (1986)

3. To show plurals of numbers, letters, and words used as words.

>   two *4*'s   some *B*'s   too many *and*'s

A Hyphen (-) Is Used—

1. When writing out compound numbers between 21 and 99.

>   twenty-three   sixty-one   ninety-ninth

2. When writing out fractions used as modifiers, but not when fractions are used as nouns.

>   two-thirds majority

But:

>   Two thirds were counted present.

3. To avoid confusing words that are spelled alike.

>   re-cover the sofa, *but* recover from the flu
>   re-lay a carpet, *but* a relay race

4. In some words, to avoid awkwardly joining letters.

>   anti-intellectual   pre-established   semi-invalid

But:

>   cooperate

5. After a prefix when the root word begins with a capital letter.

>   pre-Hispanic   mid-Pacific   un-American

6. After the prefixes *all-, ex-,* and *self-* (in most cases).

>   all-powerful   ex-classmate   self-conscious

7. Between parts of a compound adjective when it appears before the word it modifies.

>   hard-working father   up-to-date news   well-known person

But:

> Dad is hard working. It is up to date. She is well known.

8. Between parts of some compound nouns.

> father-in-law   great-grandmother   stay-at-home

But:

> attorney general   coat of arms

9. To divide a word at the end of a line. You may divide a word only between syllables—but not between all syllables in all words. There are some places where you should not divide a word, even where there is a syllable break. Here are some general guidelines for deciding where to divide words at the end of lines.

a. Do not divide words of one syllable, contractions, ab-breviations, or numbers written in figures.

> thought   width   give
> shouldn't (*not* should-n't)
> UNICEF (*not* UNI-CEF)
> 3,416,521 (*not* 3,416-521)

b. Do not divide a word if either part is a word by itself or the hyphenation could cause confusion.

> often (*not* of-ten) piety (*not* pie-ty) women (*not* wo-men)

c. Do not divide one-letter syllables or *-ed* from the rest of the word.

> amend-ment (*not* a-mendment)
> at-tached (*not* attach-ed)

d. Divide a word after a prefix or before a suffix. But do not carry over a two-letter suffix to the next line.

> trans-portation *or* transporta-tion (*not* transpor-tation)
> mostly (*not* most-ly)

e. Divide compound words between their main parts. And divide hyphenated compounds at the hyphen.

> home-coming (*not* homecom-ing)
> self-respect (*not* self-re-spect)

f. Divide between double consonants. But divide after double consonants if the root word ends in the double consonant.

> run-ning   get-ting
> pull-ing   miss-ing

g. Do not hyphenate at the end of a word where an *l* is followed by a silent *e*.

> babble (*not* bab-ble)
> people (*not* peo-ple)

Be aware that there are exceptions to the hyphenation rules. Check your dictionary whenever you are unsure. And always place the hyphen at the end of the line, not at the beginning of the next line.

> The bill passed through the House and the Sen-
> ate.

Quotation Marks (" ") Are Used—

1. To enclose all parts of a direct quote.

> "I think you should shorten this," said the teacher, "because you're running out of space."

2. To enclose quoted words or phrases within a sentence.

> My father always tells me to "get a good night's sleep and eat a hearty breakfast."

Enclose a quote within a quote in single quotation marks.

> "When I asked my father for advice, he said, 'Get a good night's sleep and eat a hearty breakfast,'" Jane explained.

3. To enclose the titles of short musical works and poems.

> "The Star-Spangled Banner"
> "To a Waterfowl"

4. Around the titles of book chapters, magazine articles, lectures, sermons, and pamphlets.

> For homework, read "The Making of Modern England" in your history book.

5. To enclose a word or phrase explained or defined by the rest of the sentence; a technical term in nontechnical writing; and slang, well-known expressions, or words whose meaning is contradicted in the sentence (irony).

> By "soon" he means tomorrow.
> You need a "declination chart" to use the compass accurately.
> The new mystery is a "thriller-diller."
> Johnny's "pursuing happiness" at the video arcade.
> The "joy of motherhood" is not found in changing diapers.

6. Before the beginning of each stanza of a quoted poem and after the last stanza.

7. Before each paragraph of continuous quoted material and after the last paragraph. Quotation marks are not used at the end of middle paragraphs. Often they are not used with single-line quotes presented by themselves between original paragraphs.

8. Commas and periods are placed inside closing quotation marks.

> "I will go now," she said, "and be back in an hour."

9. Semicolons and colons are placed outside closing quotation marks.

> She said, "I'll go to the store"; but then she stayed home.
> "To be or not to be": this is one of Shakespeare's most famous lines.

10. Question marks and exclamation points are placed inside the closing quotation marks if they belong to the quote.

> "What book are you reading?" he asked.
> "Go now!" she ordered.

But if they are not part of the quote, question marks and exclamation points go outside the quotation marks.

> Did they sing "America the Beautiful"?
> What a surprise when she said, "I'm moving"!

Parentheses ( ) Are Used—

1. To enclose additional material in a sentence.

> President Washington (1732–1799) was from Virginia.

2. To enclose sources of information within a sentence.

> Cain was jealous of Abel and killed him (Genesis 4:5–8).

3. Around numbers or letters that indicate subdivisions of a sentence.

> There will be three test parts: (1) true-false, (2) multiple choice, and (3) essay.

Brackets ([ ]) Are Used—

1. To enclose words already within parentheses.

> Shakespeare's most difficult tragedy (*Hamlet* [written about 1600]) has been performed many times.

2. To correct a direct quote that originally had a mistake.

> "The choc[o]lates were delicious," wrote my little brother.

3. To explain something within a direct quote.

> Kathy said, "When I get older [she was 4 then], I'm going to buy a dog."

4. To present stage and acting directions in plays.

> MARY [seated, with face in her hands]: I am so depressed!

Ellipses (. . . or . . . .) Are Used—

With direct quotes to show that a word or words have been left out. Use three spaced dots to show that words are missing at the beginning or within the quote. To show missing words at the end of a quote, use four spaced dots (the first dot is the period). Here are examples for the complete quote "Individual sports like gymnastics and downhill skiing are exciting and fascinating to watch."

> The announcer said, ". . . Gymnastics and downhill skiing are exciting. . . ."
> The announcer said, "Individual sports . . . are exciting and fascinating to watch."

A Slash (Solidus) Is Used—

1. Between two words to indicate that the meaning of either word could apply.

>My sister and/or brother will be home.

2. As a dividing line in dates, fractions, and abbreviations.

>5/29/68   5/8   c/o (in care of)

3. With run-in lines of poetry to show where one line ends and another begins. (Leave a little space on either side.)

>"All the world's a stage, / And all the men and women merely players. / They have their exits and their entrances: / And one man in his time plays many parts, / His acts being seven ages."

Italics or Underlining Is Used—

1. For the titles of books, plays, long poems, newspapers, and magazines.

>*The Black Stallion*　　　*Julius Caesar*　　　*Odyssey*
>The *Tuscaloosa News*　　　*Newsweek*

2. For titles of paintings and other works of art.

>*The Blue Boy*　　*Venus de Milo*

3. For names of specific ships, planes, trains, and satellites.

>*Titanic*　　*Spirit of St. Louis*　　*Orient Express*　　*Telstar*

4. For any foreign word that is not commonly used in English. These words have labels (such as Latin, French, or Italian) in the dictionary.

>The Hawaiian girl said *aloha oe* when she left.
>The party was *wunderbar,* according to our cousin.

5. For any words, letters, or numbers used as words.

>*A, an,* and *the* are articles.
>Cross your *t*'s and dot your *i*'s.
>The *7*'s in multiplication were hard, but the *10*'s were easy.

Remember that these words appear in *italics* when set in type (as in books or magazines). They are underlined when handwritten or typed.

IV

COMMON GRAMMAR AND USAGE ERRORS

Errors commonly made in grammar and usage are presented in this section, along with methods of correcting and avoiding them.

...ouis Stevenson, was first

tense

...story (took) place in th...

(are) agreement

...ng to Engla...

...he name English sa...

of South America (In...

the main characters in the sto...

Hawkins, Squire Trelawney, Dr. Livesey, Long...

Silver, Captain Smollett, and Ben Gunn. Ji...

sp.
Hawkins, the story's hero, (narates) most of the

story in the first person. He is a young

boy ~~whom~~ serves as cabin boy on the

that
...paniola, the ship ~~which~~ sails for

Common Grammar and Usage Errors

*S*ome *words and expressions are unacceptable in formal writing or speaking. This section presents many commonly misused words, phrases, and constructions. It also suggests ways to avoid them.*

Misused Words

a, an. *A* is used before words beginning with consonant sounds; *an,* before words beginning with vowel sounds (regardless of what the first letter is).

> *a* hat   *a* table   *a* car
> *an* apple   *an* hour   *an* oven

accept, except. *Accept* means "to receive willingly"; *except* means "to exclude." As a preposition, *except* means "other than."

> I will *accept* the first part of your suggestion, but I must *except* the second part.
> I jog every day *except* Sunday.

advice, advise. *Advice* is a noun; *advise,* a verb. Do not use *advise* to mean "inform" or "tell"; save it for "give notice" or "warn."

> She gave me good *advice* when she *advised* me not to hitchhike.

affect, effect. *Affect* is a verb meaning "to influence." *Effect,* as a verb, means "to cause, bring about, or accomplish"; as a noun *effect* means "a result or an accomplishment." *Affect* is never a noun.

> His presence *affected* the mood of the party.
> A new club constitution was *effected* after two weeks of meetings.
> The play had a wonderful *effect* on the audience.

aggravate, irritate. *Aggravate* means "to make an already troubled situation worse, or more serious." *Irritate* means "to annoy, exasperate, or chafe."

> Sitting in a draft *aggravated* my stiff neck.
> Some detergents can *irritate* your skin.

all the farther, all the faster. Do not use these expressions. Use *as far as* or *as fast as*.

allude, elude, illude. *Allude* means "to make an indirect reference to something." *Elude* means "to avoid or evade." *Illude* means "to deceive or trick." And don't confuse *allude* with *refer: refer* means "to make a direct reference to a specific thing."

> He *alluded* to a past time when he was young and rich.
> The teacher *referred* us to page 20 in the text.
> The criminal *eluded* the police.
> He *illuded* us into thinking he was from Great Britain.

among, between. Use *among* to show the relation of more than two persons or things; use *between* when dealing with two things (or more than two things if each is considered individually).

> We are *among* friends.
> I was standing *between* the sofa and the table.
> The railroad runs *between* Chicago, Milwaukee, and Minneapolis.

amount, number. *Amount* is used with a unified bulk or lump sum; *number* suggests separate, countable units.

> The *number* of nickels you gave doesn't add up to the *amount* the candy costs.
> The *amount* of flour here isn't enough for the *number* of cakes we need to bake.

and etc. Do not use this expression.

anticipate, expect. Use *anticipate* when you mean "to prepare for something." Use *expect* when you mean "to think something will occur."

> They *anticipated* the storm by going to a safe place.
> We *expect* the mail will be delayed.

anxious, eager. *Anxious* suggests anxiety or worry; *eager* means "looking forward to or wanting to."

>We are *anxious* about the campers' safety.
>I am *eager* to start my vacation.

anyways, anywheres. Do not use these words. Use *anyway* and *anywhere* instead.

apt, liable, likely. *Apt* suggests fitness or suitability; *liable* suggests obligation; and *likely* indicates probability.

>She is an *apt* musician.
>They were held *liable* for the damage.
>The rain is *likely* to arrive here this evening.

awhile, a while. *Awhile* is an adverb; *while* (as in *a while*) is a noun. Use *a while* after prepositions (*for a while, after a while*).

>Work *awhile* longer, and I'll help you.
>She stood there for *a while*.

bad, badly. *Bad* is an adjective; *badly,* an adverb. Use *bad* after linking verbs (*is, feels, tastes*).

>He was a *bad* boy today.
>The engine misfired *badly*.
>She feels *bad* about missing the concert.

beside, besides. *Beside* means "alongside of"; *besides* means "in addition to."

>He sat *beside* me.
>*Besides* the mortgage, Dad has car payments to make.

biannual, biennial. *Biannual* means "twice a year"; *biennial* means "once every two years."

>We received the *biannual* reports in January and July.
>We received the *biennial* reports in 1984 and 1986.

bursted, bust, busted. Never use *bursted;* the past tense of *burst* is *burst*. *Bust* and *busted* are slang uses of burst; don't use them.

>The pipe *burst* today. The pipe *is bursting* now.
>The pipe *burst* yesterday. This pipe *has burst* before.

can, may. *Can* means "is able to." *May* means "has permission to."

> You *can* sketch well when you take your time.
> After you have put everything away, you *may* leave.

capital, capitol. Use *capital* (with an *a*) when referring to money, upper-case letters, a city in which a government is located, or crimes punishable by death. Use *capitol* (with an *o*) only when referring to buildings where legislatures meet.

> *Capitol* has a *capital C* if it means the building in which the Congress of the United States meets.

contact, contacted. These are much overused terms. Replace them with *call, consult, telephone, see,* or *write.*

credible, creditable, credulous. *Credible* means "believable." *Creditable* means "worthy of esteem or praise." *Credulous* means "gullible."

> His account of the situation was *credible.*
> He made a *creditable* contribution to the project.
> *Credulous* people believe everything that they are told.

data. *Data* is the plural form of the Latin word *datum.* It can be used as a collective singular noun when referring to a body of information as a unit.

> The *data* [figures] in this chart are confusing.
> The *data* [information] was available to everyone.

different than, different from. Use *different from.*

> Elementary school is *different from* junior high.

disinterested, uninterested. *Disinterested* means "unbiased"; *uninterested,* "having no interest in."

> The argument was settled by a *disinterested* party.
> I am *uninterested* in your argument.

doubt but, help but. Do not use these expressions.

> I don't *doubt that* you are right.
> I can't *help* worrying.

due to, because of. Do not use *due to* for *because of, owing to,* or *on account of. Due to* is correct after a linking verb, or as an adjective following a noun.

Wrong: *Due to* heavy traffic, I was late.
Correct: *Because of* heavy traffic, I was late.
            My tardiness was *due to* heavy traffic.
            Deena got pneumonia *due to* a bad cold.

each . . . are. This is an agreement error. *Each* implies one and takes a singular verb. Plural words used in phrases that modify *each* do not change the number of the verb.

Each student *was* promoted.
Each of the students *was* promoted.

emigrate, immigrate. *Emigrate* means "to move out of a country"; *immigrate,* "to move into a country."

They *emigrated* from Ireland. She *immigrated* to Canada.

enthuse. Do not use the verb *enthuse.* Use *showed enthusiasm* or *was enthusiastic.*

Wrong: He *enthused* about the new project.
Correct: He *showed enthusiasm* about the new project.
            He *was enthusiastic* about the new project.

etc. Avoid using this expression in writing. Instead, say specifically what you mean.

Weak: Use books, magazines, etc., to do your research.
Better: Use books, magazines, and other library materials to do your research.

farther, further. Use *farther* to suggest a distance that can be measured. Use *further* to show a greater degree, extent, quantity, or time. *Further* also means "moreover" and "in addition to."

We walked *farther* than we had to.
We can discuss this matter *further* tomorrow.
The baby's tired and, *further,* she's hungry.

fewer, less. *Fewer* applies to things that can be numbered or counted. *Less* applies to things in bulk, in the abstract, or in degree and value.

There are *fewer* houses here because there is *less* land.

formally, formerly. *Formally* means "in a formal manner"; *formerly* means "in the past."

> Jan Smith, who *formerly* attended Paul Junior High School, was *formally* graduated from Lincoln Junior High School last spring.

good, well. *Good* is an adjective; *well,* an adverb. *Well* acts as an adjective only when describing someone's health.

> I had a *good* time; the dinner had been planned *well.*
> She felt *good* about the project, but she did not feel *well* enough to go to work on it.

had best, had better, had ought. Do not use these verbs. Use *ought to* or *should* instead.

> Those children *ought to (should)* behave.

hanged, hung. People are *hanged;* things (pictures, clothes) are *hung.*

> The vigilantes *hanged* an innocent sheepherder.
> Grandfather *hung* my picture in his den.

hardly, scarcely. *Hardly* means "done with difficulty" or "barely able to." *Scarcely* suggests "not enough."

> I could *hardly* push the power mower; I had *scarcely* any energy left.

have got. Use just *have.*

> "I *have* it [not I*'ve got* it]."

imply, infer. *Imply* means "to suggest or hint at"; *infer* means "to draw a conclusion."

> He *implied* that he would vote against it.
> I *inferred* from my mother's behavior that something was wrong.

in, into. *In* suggests being inside; *into* suggests the act of entering.

> She was sitting *in* my chair when I walked *into* the room.

inside of, off of, outside of. The *of* is unnecessary with these prepositions.

> I keep my wallet *inside* my purse.
> He stood *outside* the door.

irregardless, disregardless. Do not use these words. Use *regardless.*

> They played *regardless* of the rain.

is when, is where. Do not use these phrases for definitions or explanations.

> **Wrong:** Writing *is when* you put your thoughts on paper.
> **Correct:** Writing *is* putting your thoughts on paper.

its, it's. *Its* is the possessive of *it; it's* is the contraction for *it is.*

> *It's* sad that the dog broke *its* foot.

kind, sort, type. These are singular nouns and must be modified by singular adjectives.

> this kind *but* these kinds
> that type *but* those types

kind of a, sort of a, type of a. Remove the *a.* And do not use *kind of, sort of,* or *type of* in place of *somewhat, rather,* or *almost.*

> What *kind of* material are you using?
> I'm *somewhat* undecided.

leave, let. *Leave* means "to depart" or "to allow to remain in a certain condition." *Let* means "to allow, enable, or not interfere with."

> I will *leave* the computer and *let* you use it.
> *Leave* the window open.

lie, lay. *Lie* means "to recline"; the principal parts of this verb are *lie, lay, lain. Lying* is the present participle. *Lay* means "to put or place"; the principal parts of this verb are *lay, laid, laid. Laying* is the present participle.

Lie	Lay
Lie down and rest.	Will they *lay* the tile?
I *lay* down yesterday to rest.	They *laid* the tile yesterday.
I *had lain* down to rest.	They *have laid* tile before.
I *was lying* on the couch.	They *are laying* the tile.

like, as. *As* is a conjunction; use *as* to join clauses. *Like* is a preposition; *like* with a noun or pronoun forms a prepositional phrase.

> I did the assignment *as* I was instructed to do it (or *as* instructed).
> My sister looks *like* me. I look *like* Aunt Ruth.

loan, lend. *Loan* is a noun; *lend* is a verb.

> I will *lend* you the money, but you must pay this *loan* in full.

lots, lots of, a whole lot. Use *many, much,* or *a great deal* in place of these expressions.

of. Used incorrectly for *have* after auxiliary verbs.

> **Wrong:** would *of,* could *of,* should *of*
> **Correct:** would *have,* could *have,* should *have*

perform, preform. *Perform* means "to carry out or to give a performance"; *preform* means "to form or shape beforehand."

> The orchestra *performed* beautifully.
> The patio is made of *preformed* concrete.

practicable, practical. *Practicable* means "capable of being put into practice"; *practical* means "being useful or successful."

> The new rules seem *practicable.*
> She always finds *practical* solutions for our problems.

principal, principle. *Principal* as a noun refers to a sum of money, or a person or thing of first importance; as an adjective, *principal* means "first, chief, or main." *Principle* is a noun meaning "a law, code, doctrine, or rule."

> The *principal* of the loan was $70,000.
> Our *principal* is Ms. Smith.
> Getting good grades is my *principal* goal this school year.
> She is a leader with high *principles.*

raise, rise. *Raise* is a transitive verb requiring an object; its principal parts are *raise, raised, raised.* Its present participle is *raising. Rise,* an intransitive verb, does not require an object; its principal parts are *rise, rose, risen.* Its present participle is *rising.*

> I *raised* tomatoes and corn.
> Please *rise* to sing the school anthem.

real, really. *Real* is an adjective meaning "genuine or having reality." *Really* is an adverb meaning "actually or truly."

> The stone looked like a *real* diamond, but it *really* was a fake.

reason is because. Do not use this construction. Instead, say *reason is* or *reason is that.*

> **Wrong:**   The *reason* why I am late *is because* the car stalled.
> **Correct:**   The *reason* why I am late *is* complicated.
> **Correct:**   The *reason* why I am late *is that* the car stalled.

respectfully, respectively. *Respectfully* means "in a respectful manner." *Respectively* means "each in the order given."

> I am *respectfully* observing Memorial Day.
> I talked *respectively* to Alex, Donald, and Gordon.

seen, saw. The principal parts of *see* are *see, saw, seen.* The present participal is *seeing.*

> **Wrong:**   I *seen* them at the store.   We *have saw* the movie.
> **Correct:**   I *saw* them at the store.   We *have seen* the movie.

shall, will. Use *shall* with *I* and *we* in the future tense, and in directives. Use *will* with *he, she, it,* and *they,* and with *I* and *we* when giving a promise.

> I *shall* go to work; she *will* go to school.
> The police *shall* have the authority to confiscate stolen goods.
> I *will* do all that I can to help you.

sit, set. *Sit* means "place oneself"; *set* means "to put or place something."

> *Sit* down and rest awhile. I will *set* the box on the floor.

so. Do not use *so* in place of *so that, therefore,* or *thus.* And do not use *so* to mean "very": *so* kind, *so* terrible. Use a stronger word instead.

> **Wrong:** I wish to go *so* I can meet her, too.
> **Correct:** I wish to go *so that* I can meet her, too.

> **Wrong:** That is *so* silly.
> **Correct:** That is *ridiculous.*

that, which. *That* is often used to begin restrictive clauses (clauses that are necessary to the meaning of the sentence). *Which* is used to begin many nonrestrictive clauses (clauses that simply provide additional information).

> The house *that* I liked was not for sale. [restrictive]
> My house, *which* is old, needs many repairs. [nonrestrictive]

then, also. These words are adverbs. Do not use them instead of conjunctions.

> **Wrong:** He ate breakfast, *then* went to work.
> We enjoy skiing, *also* skating.
> **Correct:** He ate breakfast *and* then went to work.
> We enjoy skiing *and* skating.

there, their, they're. *There* means "in or at that place." *Their* is a possessive pronoun. *They're* is a contraction for *they are.*

> Connie parked the car *there.*
> *Their* house was custom-built.
> *They're* going to leave soon.

to, too, two. *To* is a preposition (*to* the store) and the word that introduces an infinitive (*to* walk). *Too* is an adverb meaning "also" or "more than what is proper or enough" (me, *too; too* hot). *Two* is the number (*two* cats).

try and. Do not use *try and.* Use *try to.*

> **Wrong:** I will *try and* finish the painting today.
> **Correct:** I will *try to* finish the painting today.

type. Do not use as a substitute for *type of.*

> **Wrong:** I would like to buy this *type* dress.
> **Correct:** I would like to buy this *type of* dress.

unique. *Unique* means "the only one of its kind" or "without equal." Do not use *more* or *most* with *unique*.

> **Wrong:** Those are *most unique* earrings.
> **Correct:** Those are *unique* earrings.

very. *Very* is an overused adverb. Try to use more specific modifiers, or use words that are strong in themselves. This same advice applies to *so, surely, too, extremely, indeed*.

> **Weak:** She sings *very* well.
> **Improved:** She sings *beautifully*.
> She is a *talented singer*.

while. *While* means "during the time that." Do not use *while* in place of *although, and, but,* or *whereas*.

> **Wrong:** The days were hot, *while* the nights were cool.
> **Correct:** The days were hot, *but* the nights were cool.
> *While* you were on vacation, we won the championship.

who, whom. Use *who* as a subject. Use *whom* as an object.

> That is the boy *who* threw the rock. [*who* is the subject of *threw*]
> The girl for *whom* I bought the gift was delighted. [*whom* is the object of the preposition *for*]
> My mother, *who* is often late, came early. [*who* is the subject of *is*]

Misused Constructions

Misused grammatical constructions are confusing. Here are some explanations of problems you can avoid.

Agreement Problems

Subject-Verb Agreement

A verb must agree with its subject in number and person.

Number: The *paper was* at the door. [singular]
The *papers were* on my desk. [plural]

Singular	Plural
Person: *I am* at home.	*We are* at home.
You are at home.	*You are* at home.
He, she, it is at home.	*They are* at home.

Here are some additional reminders about subject-verb agreement.

1. When other parts of a sentence come between the subject and the verb, these parts do not change the person or the number of the verb.

> The *boys* who had a good time at the party *are* now playing softball.
> The *report* about leases and contracts *was* distributed.

2. Inverting the order of the subject and verb does not affect agreement.

> In the trunk *were piles* of money. [*Piles were*. . . .]

3. Some nouns are plural in form but singular in meaning and therefore take singular verbs: *news, measles, United Nations.*

> The *news was* bad.
> The *United Nations is* located in New York.

Some nouns are plural in form but can be either singular or plural, depending on their meaning in the sentence. Some of these nouns are *economics, athletics, politics, ethics.*

> *Athletics* keep the nation in shape.
> What is *athletics* if not a way of life?

4. Two or more subjects joined by *and* take a plural verb.

> The *baby* and the *dog love* attention. [They love. . . .]

If the two subjects form a single idea or are thought of as a unit, they should take a singular verb.

> *Macaroni* and *cheese is* my favorite dish. [It is. . . .]

5. Singular subjects joined by *or* or *nor* take a singular verb.

> Either the *house* or the *garage is* on fire.

If the subjects joined by *or* or *nor* differ in number or person, the verb agrees with the subject nearer the verb.

> Neither the *lamp* nor the *bulbs were* working.
> Either the *trees* or the *lawn needs* cutting.

6. A collective noun takes a singular verb when the group is regarded as a unit. But a collective noun takes a plural verb when emphasis is placed on the individual members of the group.

> The *audience* was applauding. [*applauding* together]
> The *audience were* arriving. [*arriving* separately]

Pronoun Agreement

We have already seen that pronouns used as subjects must agree with their verbs. Pronouns must also agree with their antecedents. Here are some rules for making pronouns agree with their verbs and their antecedents.

1. When using indefinite pronouns as subjects be careful to choose the correct form of the verb. The following indefinite pronouns are considered to be singular and take singular verbs: *each, either, neither,* and all pronouns ending in *-body, -one,* or *-thing.*

> *Each* of these apples *is* spoiled.
> *Nobody wants* to be sick.
> *Everyone is* here.

These indefinite pronouns are considered to be plural and take plural verbs: *both, few, many, several.*

> *Both* of you *are* going to succeed.
> *Many are* called, but *few are* chosen.

All, any, most, none, and *some* can be either singular or plural, depending on their meaning in the sentence. When the pronoun refers to one thing or to a quantity as a whole, use a singular verb. When the pronoun refers to a number of individual items, use a plural verb.

Some of the money *was* missing. [singular]
Some of their friends *were* there. [plural]
All of my hope *is* gone. [singular]
All of you *are* invited. [plural]

2. When the subject is a relative pronoun (*who, which, that*), the verb should agree with the pronoun's antecedent.

> She is the student *who speaks* Spanish. [student speaks]
> The dogs *that were barking* are quiet now. [dogs were barking]

3. A pronoun agrees with its antecedent in gender, number, and person.

> The *woman* picked up *her* groceries.
> The *women* picked up *their* groceries.

Be especially careful when the pronoun's antecedent is an indefinite pronoun. Follow the rules given above for deciding if the indefinite pronoun is singular or plural; then make the other pronoun agree with the indefinite pronoun.

> *Neither* of the girls is wearing *her* coat.
> *All* of the girls are wearing *their* coats.

4. When the antecedent is a collective noun, the pronoun is either singular or plural—depending on whether the collective noun is singular or plural in the sentence.

> The *committee* made *its* decision.
> The *committee* discussed the matter among *themselves*

Faulty Pronoun References

Every pronoun must have an antecedent. Place pronouns as close as possible to their antecedents so that it is clear what word the pronoun refers back to.

1. Avoid confusing references. A reader will be confused if a sentence contains two possible antecedents for a pronoun.

> **Confusing:**   After Michael talked to Bill, *he* was angry.
> **Clear:**   After Michael talked to Bill, *Bill* was angry.
>   *or* Michael was angry after he talked to Bill.

2. Avoid vague references. Vague references occur when the antecedent of a pronoun is not actually stated. Using *they, this, that,* and *which* to refer to an entire statement (rather than to one noun) is a common form of vague reference.

> **Vague:** I had not finished the report, *which* irritated Mr. Brown.
>
> **Clear:** The fact that I had not finished the report irritated Mr. Brown.
>
> My failure to finish the report irritated Mr. Brown.

3. Avoid the indefinite use of *it, they,* and *you.*

> **Confusing:** In the first act, *it* shows Hamlet's character.
>
> **Clear:** In the first act, Hamlet's character is shown.
>
> In the first act, Hamlet shows his character.

Shifts in Point of View

In writing, the point of view should be as consistent as possible. Shifts in point of view include changes in number, subject, tense, and voice. There are of course times when you do need to change the point of view. But frequent and unnecessary shifts are confusing.

1. Avoid unnecessary shifts in number (singular and plural).

> **Wrong:** *Plants are* lovely, but *it requires* much care.
>
> **Correct:** *Plants are* lovely, but *they require* much care.

2. Avoid unnecessary shifts in the subjects in sentences.

> **Wrong:** If *you* do your research, *it* will be a good paper.
>
> **Correct:** If *you* do your research, *you* will write a good paper.

3. Avoid unnecessary shifts in tense (present, past, future).

> **Wrong:** Jack *came* home and *took* off his jacket. He *walks* to his room and *changes* clothes. Ten minutes later, he *was* ready to eat dinner.
>
> **Correct:** Jack *came* home and *took* off his jacket. He *walked* to his room and *changed* clothes. Ten minutes later, he *was* ready to eat dinner.

4. Avoid unnecessary shifts in voice (active and passive).

Wrong: He *did* good work, but no special credit *was received*.

Correct: He *did* good work, but he *received* no special credit.

Improper Parts of Speech

Words that belong to one part of speech are sometimes incorrectly used as another part of speech. Here are some examples of using the incorrect part of speech:

Nouns incorrectly used as verbs: *author* a book, *host* a program

Adjectives incorrectly used as adverbs: played *good, real* pretty

Sentence Faults

Sentence faults occur when you write sentences that are incomplete or when you improperly run sentences together.

Sentence Fragments

A sentence fragment is an incomplete sentence. If you put a period at the end of a phrase or a subordinate clause, you will have a fragment. Phrases and subordinate clauses cannot stand alone. You can correct a sentence fragment by joining it to a sentence.

Fragment: *After going to college for four years.* My brother was ready to teach.

Correct: After going to college for four years, my brother was ready to teach.

Fragment: I was late for school. *Although I awoke earlier than usual.*

Correct: I was late for school, although I awoke earlier than usual.

Sometimes you can add words or change wording to make the fragment a complete sentence in itself.

Fragment: Watching the election results all night.

Correct: My family was watching the election results all night.

Fragment: One of my friends who lost her ring in the swimming pool.

Correct: One of my friends lost her ring in the swimming pool.

Run-on Sentences

A run-on sentence is two or more sentences incorrectly connected. A comma alone cannot properly join sentences. These are run-on sentences because only a comma appears between the two clauses. This error is called a comma splice.

Run-on: The team managers worked hard, they did a good job.

Run-on: The committee is scheduled to meet tomorrow, it has many matters to discuss.

Run-on: Classes started on September 5, however, I did not arrive until September 7.

Run-on sentences can be corrected in several ways:

1. Make two separate sentences.

The team managers worked hard. They did a good job.

2. Use a semicolon between the clauses.

Classes started on September 5; however, I did not register until September 7.

3. Use a conjunction between the clauses (such as *and, but, or,* or *nor*).

The team managers worked hard, *and* they did a good job.

4. Make one of the statements into a phrase or a subordinate clause.

Scheduled to meet tomorrow, the committee has many matters to discuss.

Another error is to run sentences together with no punctuation at all between them. These run-together sentences must also be separated or properly connected.

Wrong:	I spent a month's allowance for this dress I like the style.
Correct:	I spent a month's allowance for this dress. I like the style.
	I spent a month's allowance for this dress because I like the style.
	I spent a month's allowance for this dress; I like the style.
Wrong:	Why are you leaving now wait I'll walk home with you.
Correct:	Why are you leaving now? Wait! I'll walk home with you.
	Why are you leaving now? Wait and I'll walk home with you.

Split Constructions

Unnecessarily splitting infinitives, separating subjects from verbs, or separating parts of a verb phrase are errors called split constructions. Here is a list with examples of split constructions to avoid:

1. Avoid split infinitives. An infinitive is *to* plus a verb (*to walk, to think*). Putting other words between *to* and the verb is often awkward.

Awkward:	To be or *to* not *be:* that is the question.
Better:	To be or not *to be:* that is the question.
Awkward:	We had *to* without any preparation or warning *pack* our belongings.
Better:	Without any preparation or warning, we had *to pack* our belongings.

2. Avoid unnecessarily separating a subject and its verb or a verb and its object. Keeping these basic sentence parts together usually makes your writing clearer.

Awkward:	*Mary,* in one bounding leap, *cleared* the fence. [subject and verb separated]
Awkward:	Mary *cleared,* in one bounding leap, *the fence.* [verb and object separated]
Better:	*Mary cleared the fence* in one bounding leap.

3. Do not separate a preposition from its object.

Awkward:	He walked *into,* since he was in the neighbor-hood, *the museum.*
Better:	Since he was in the neighborhood, he walked *into the museum.*

4. Do not separate the parts of a verb phrase.

Awkward:	Mary *has,* although you would not think so, *been* ill.
Better:	Mary *has been* ill, although you would not think so.
Awkward:	I *might have,* if you had not opposed me, *bought* the portable phone.
Better:	If you had not opposed me, I *might have bought* the portable phone.

Faulty Parallel Constructions

Parallel construction means expressing two or more related ideas in the same grammatical form. To make a pair of ideas parallel, you would state both ideas in the same structure—in the same kind of words, phrases, clauses, or sentences. You should also use parallel structure in a series of items joined by *and* or *or.* Here are some examples of parallel structure:

Words:	*Working* and *playing* are both important.
Phrases:	Both *at home* and *at school* she is well organized.
Clauses:	I will cut the grass *when my back is better* and *when the mower is repaired.*
Sentences:	*Our neighbor to the south has a brick house and a well-kept lawn. Our neighbor to the north has a wood-frame house and a weedy lawn.*

Here are some examples of faulty parallelism, along with some ways to correct them:

Wrong:	*To write* was easier for her than *talking.*
Correct:	*Writing* was easier for her than *talking.*
Wrong:	He enjoys playing *golf, tennis,* and *to play softball.*

Correct: He enjoys playing *golf, tennis,* and *softball.*

Wrong: *Having checked our bags* and *since we had said good-bye,* we boarded the plane.

Correct: Since we *had checked our bags* and *had said good-bye,* we boarded the plane.

Wrong: The animal shelter *cares for unwanted animals* and *is trying to find homes for them.*

Correct: The animal shelter *cares for unwanted animals* and *tries to find homes for them.*

Problems with Modifiers

Whenever you use modifying words, phrases, and clauses, be sure that the relationship between the modifier and the word it modifies is clear. Avoid the following common problems with modifiers.

Dangling Modifiers

Adjective phrases and clauses that are not connected to any word or phrase in the sentence are called dangling modifiers. These danglers cause confusion. The reader does not know what they modify. Here are examples of dangling modifiers, along with some ways to correct them:

Dangling: *Hanging the curtains,* the rod slipped and hit him on the head.

Correct: When *he was hanging the curtains,* the rod slipped and hit him on the head.

Dangling: *Young and alone,* the dark can be frightening.

Correct: *Young and alone, she* was frightened by the dark.

    Young and alone, a child can be frightened by the dark.

Dangling: *To complete the project on time,* the typewriter must be repaired.

Correct: *To complete the project on time, I* must have the typewriter repaired.

    If the project is to be completed on time, the typewriter must be repaired.

Squinting Modifiers

An adverb that is placed between two verbs—both of which it could modify—is called a squinting modifier.

> The hammer that he was waving *menacingly* fell to the floor.

Look at *menacingly* one time, and it seems to refer to *was waving*. Look at it again, and it seems to refer to *fell*. In other words, the modifier, *menacingly,* squints at both verbs. The writer probably meant:

> The hammer that he was *menacingly* waving fell to the floor.

Misplaced Modifiers

These are phrases or clauses that are not placed close enough to the word they modify. They sometimes appear to modify a word other than the word they are intended to modify.

Of the three incorrect modifier constructions, the misplaced modifier is the easiest one to correct. Look at these sentences. The first sentence in each group has a misplaced modifier; the second has the modifier in the correct place.

> **Misplaced:** Mary admitted to her mother *with a sad face* that she had failed the chemistry examination. [seems to modify *mother*]
>
> **Clear:** *With a sad face,* Mary admitted to her mother that she had failed the chemistry examination.
>
> **Misplaced:** He keeps the awards he won *at school in his bedroom.*
>
> **Clear:** *In his bedroom,* he keeps the awards he won *at school.*
>
> The awards he won *at school* are kept *in his bedroom.*

Avoiding Clichés

Clichés, or overused words and expressions, are a part of everyday language. They can seem colorful and fun to use. Have you ever passed a test *by the skin of your teeth?* You may have waited *with bated breath* for your grade. *In the final analysis,* you would have been *down in the dumps* if you hadn't passed.

Don't let anyone *put words in your mouth.* Clichés are worn out. Use your own words to express your thoughts. This is one reason for avoiding clichés.

Another reason is that many clichés are no fun at all. They are boring and overstuffed. People use them to sound official or smart. Would you and your friends ever *endeavor* to *inaugurate* the *widespread use* of seat belts? You'd more likely *try* to *begin using* seat belts *regularly.*

An important language goal is learning to say things in the fewest words possible. Don't waste anyone's time. Many clichés are wordy. That's the third reason to avoid them. *It's a cinch* that you and your friends would never *cooperate together* when you could *definitely* simply *cooperate.* You may have *in the neighborhood of* ten problems to discuss. But discussing *about* ten problems will get the same results. A *budding genius* may be able to solve them all, but a *genius* could do the same.

Exercise your vocabulary skills. Replace clichés with original words that fit your meaning. When it is necessary, rearrange your sentences. Or add a twist to a worn-out phrase, making it your own. You'll find that there's usually more than one way to *skin a cliché.*

There are many clichés. Here are some common ones with words that can replace them. *It goes without saying* that your *best bet* is to *put your nose to the grindstone* and learn these replacements.

Cliché	Replacement
abreast of the times	current
according to Hoyle	by the rules
according to the record	the record shows that
aching void	emptiness
acid test	conclusive test
acknowledge defeat	admit defeat
after all is said and done	really
ahead of schedule	early
all in all	altogether
almost never	seldom
along the same lines	similarly
and like that	in that way
are of the opinion	think; believe
as luck would have it	fortunately; unfortunately
at a loss for words	speechless
at the present time	today; now
bathed in tears	sobbing
best bet	best decision
bitter end	end
bolt from the blue	surprise
bottom line	total; goal
budding genius	genius
busy as a bee	extremely busy
by and large	generally
by force of circumstances	because
by leaps and bounds	fast
by the skin of one's teeth	barely
captain of the ship	head
center of attention	focus
checkered career	bad record
clinging vine	dependent person
close to nature	natural
colossal mistake	bad error
come into conflict	conflict (verb)
compare favorably	compare well
conduct an investigation	investigate
conspicuous by one's absence	missed
cook one's goose	harm; ruin

Cliché	Replacement
cooperate together	cooperate
cost the sum of	cost
create the possibility	enable
deadly earnest	serious
doom to failure	insure failure
down in the dumps	miserable
due in large measure to	due largely to
each and every	all
endeavor	try
epic struggle	prolonged fight
equal to the occasion	able
every fiber of one's being	completely
fabricate	lie
fair sex	women
familiar landmark	well-known landmark
few and far between	rare
first and foremost	first
fit as a fiddle	fit
fly off the handle	rage
footprints in the sands of time	past events
for a period of a week	for a week
for all intents and purposes	seemingly
for the purpose of	in order to; to
free as the breeze	free; carefree
get down to brass tacks	get serious
give encouragement to	encourage
give rise to	cause
go without saying	be obvious
goodly number	many
green as grass	green
green with envy	envious
have need for	need
heartfelt gratitude	thanks
heart's content	satisfaction
heated argument	serious argument
hold promise	look promising
holy state of matrimony	marriage
in a most careful manner	meticulously

Cliché	Replacement
in all cases	always
in hot soup	in trouble
in one fell swoop	in one step
in terms of	regarding
in the amount of	for
in the bag	certain
in the depths of despair	depressed
in the event that	if
in the final analysis	finally
in the near future	soon
in the neighborhood of	about
in this day and age	today, now
inaugurate	begin
indigenous	native
initial	first
iron will	determination
irony of fate	irony
it goes without saying	obviously
it should be understood	understand that
it stands to reason	logically
it's a cinch	definitely
knock the tar out of	beat
large number of	many
last but not least	last
last straw	end
like a bull in a china shop	clumsy; clumsily
like an old shoe	worn out
long-felt want	always wanted
look for all the world like	look like
majority of	most of
make inquiries regarding	ask
mantle of snow	layer of snow
maximum	most
method in one's madness	method
minimum	least
month of Sundays	long time
need no introduction	be well-known
nip in the bud	stop

Cliché	Replacement
no one of right mind	normally, no one
none the worse for wear	in good condition
of a confidential nature	confidential
optimum	best
paramount issue	critical issue
picturesque scene	lovely scene
pleasing prospect	good idea
powers that be	authorities
promising future	likely success
put one's nose to the grindstone	work hard
put words in one's mouth	influence
race, color, or creed	origin, beliefs
rant and rave	rave
reign supreme	rule
right and proper	correct
sadder but wiser	experienced
safe to say	reasonable
sea of faces	crowd
self-made person	entrepreneur
significantly reduce	greatly reduce
skeleton in the closet	secret
skin alive	punish
spill the beans	blurt
strong as an ox	powerful
stubborn as a mule	obstinate
sturdy as an oak	strong
substantial portion	many, much
take into consideration	think about
take into custody	arrest
take one's word for	believe
take the easy way out	find an easy solution
than meets the eye	than is obvious
thanking you in advance	thank you for
thereby hangs the tale	that's the reason
time marches on	time passes
time of one's life	best time
too funny for words	hilarious

Cliché	Replacement
upset the applecart	disturb
utilize	use
venture a suggestion	suggest
walk of life	career
way of life	beliefs
weaker sex	women
wheel of fortune	fate
where angels fear to tread	where there's danger
widespread use	regular use; regularly
with bated breath	nervously
without further delay	immediately
words fail to express	I can't describe
wreak havoc	bring disaster

Index